Handbook of

# Quality Control of Dairy and Meat Products

# Handbook of Quality Control of Dairy and Meat Products

Sudhi Ranjan Garg

Vijay J. Jadhav

BIOTECH

2026

BIOTECH BOOKS

Reprint 2026

Sudhi Ranjan Garg

Vijay J. Jadhav

ISBN 978-81-7622-243-3



*Published by*
**BIOTECH BOOKS**
4762-63/23, Ansari Road, Darya Ganj,
New Delhi-110002 (India)
Phone: 23262132
E-mail: biotechbooks@yahoo.co.in

*Laser Typesetting by :* Deep Graphics, Delhi

PRINTED IN INDIA

## Contents

# Preface

Dairy and meat products have a substantial contribution in food security of a country. The standards of hygiene during production and highly perishable nature of the animal products influence the product safety, keeping quality, economics and acceptability, particularly in the developing countries with warm climates. Food safety is an increasingly important public health issue that has rising consumer concern all over the world. National and international agencies are constantly intensifying their efforts to improve food safety and quality everywhere. Strict food quality control measures are necessary at all stages of the food supply chain beginning with the primary production, through processing, storage, distribution and consumption to ensure that food supplies are nutritious and safe with good shelf-life.

Inspection of the food processing plants and food establishments, collection of food samples and laboratory analysis of the samples by the food regulatory agencies is indispensable to establish that necessary control measures for food quality and safety are taken by the manufacturers and distributors. It is quite essential to provide documentary evidence that the food of a particular lot is wholesome, hazard-free and fit for human consumption. This is particularly so while dealing with the export or import of foods because it may be mandatory in the international trade to follow the international standards, guidelines, and other recommendations for food quality and safety.

The major hazards in foods include: (i) Microbiological hazards such as pathogenic microorganisms, (ii) chemical hazards like toxic chemicals and adulterants, and (iii) physical hazards like dirt, hair, insects etc. Inspection of food establishments involves a detailed examination of premises, production facilities, food products, storage facilities, and the methods of handling and transport of the products to gain an insight to the food production practices and management in respect of food quality. Laboratory analysis of food samples, on the other hand, checks the quality and safety of the product and gives a detailed report. It helps in comparing the results with the prescribed specifications and, thus, in deciding the acceptability of the food product. It is utmost important that the task of inspection and laboratory analysis is accomplished by skilled persons using reliable and prescribed procedures to avoid any subsequent dispute.

This handbook is a humble attempt to elaborate the procedures and techniques of inspection and analysis of dairy and meat products in a simple but systematic manner. Regulatory guidelines concerning different kinds of hazards associated with these products have also been mentioned at appropriate places. It will not only assist the readers to make unwavering judgement about the quality of the product but will also make this handbook an indispensable reference material. Simultaneously, enough space for practice and recording the real-time observations in the handbook is certain to raise the confidence level of the users. The readers shall find the handbook really convenient and handy not only during studies but also as a refresher source throughout their career.

Sudhi Ranjan Garg
Vijay J. Jadhav

Module 1

# Sanitary collection of milk samples and rapid quality evaluation tests

Wholesome and safe milk supply to the consumers necessitates its quality evaluation at different stages of production and marketing. Therefore, milk is subjected to different tests in order to find out its chemical composition and microbiological quality. Some of these tests are quite rapid while others require lengthy protocols to follow that are time consuming. Even the most careful analysis becomes useless if the collection of sample for examination is faulty and inaccurate. Improper samples cause deviation from true values of the results of the analytical parameters. This in turn leads to wrong interpretations about the quality of the product resulting in either rejection of the product of acceptable quality or may result in the acceptance of inferior product. In both the cases, there is loss to the society, either in terms of money or in terms of health hazards to the consumers. It is, therefore, quite important that samples should be collected accurately according to the established guidelines and procedures.

## 1.1 Sanitary collection of milk samples for chemical and microbiological examination

### 1.1.1 General guidelines for sample collection

A sample should be collected by an authorized, qualified, trained and experienced person. It is also necessary to ensure that the said person is free from infectious diseases.

The purpose of sample collection should be known to the person who is engaged for this task i.e. whether the sample is meant for chemical examination or for bacteriological examination. This is important as the procedures, equipment and the method of transportation depend upon the type of analysis of the sample.

Thorough mixing of milk should be carried out before collecting sample in order to ensure that the sample is true representative of the whole lot.

While mixing the milk in a container, violent mixing should be avoided since it causes churning of fat globules and generation of air bubbles which influence the results of analysis.

Extra care should be taken while collecting the sample of frozen milk because its composition does not remain uniform throughout. Usually frozen portion is rich in water whereas the liquid portion is rich in solids. Therefore, frozen milk must be warmed to a temperature of 40°C in a water bath prior to collecting sample.

The milk samples meant for microbiological analysis should invariably be transported in chilled condition (in ice box or in refrigerator) whereas, the samples meant for chemical analysis can be preserved by adding 40% formaldehyde at the rate of 0.1 ml per 30 ml of milk. Other preservatives include potassium dichromate (0.5 ml of 14% solution per 250 ml milk), sodium azide (80 mg per 100 ml milk) and bronopol i.e. 2-bromo-2-nitro-1,3-propanediol (20 mg per 100 ml).

Each sample container should be sealed and labeled and should be accompanied with a report documenting the particulars of date, place, time, name and designation of sampling official and the precise method of sampling.

The report should be signed by the sampling official and the witnesses.

Samples should be taken in duplicate, one is sent to the laboratory for analysis while the other may be stored for any further use.

The collected milk samples should be dispatched to laboratory immediately because physical, chemical and microbiological changes affect the quality of milk.

The samples should be analysed without wasting time on arrival of the samples.

### 1.1.2 Sampling equipments

#### *Plunger*

A plunger is used to mix the milk in the container before collecting a sample. It has sufficient area to produce adequate movement of the product and it is light in weight for the operator to be able to move it rapidly through liquid milk. Thc Burcau of Indian Standards (BIS) recommends that a plunger suitable for mixing milk in the can or bucket should have a disc of 150 mm diameter which is perforated having six holes each of 12.5 mm diameter size on a pitch circle of 100 mm diameter. It is fixed centrally to a metal rod of one meter length having loop handle. The plunger suitable for agitating milk in the road or rail tankers should have a rod of length not less than 1.8 m and fitted with a 300 mm diameter disc perforated with 12 holes each of 30 mm diameter on a pitch circle of 225 mm diameter. It is usually made up of stainless steel, aluminium, tinned iron or any appropriate metal which does not adversely react with the milk.

#### *Sampling dipper*

A dipper is used to collect a measured quantity of milk sample. It consists of a small cup fixed to one end of a long handle. The BIS recommends that a dipper should have a solid handle of minimum 150 mm length and the cup of 80 ml capacity. The body of the sampling dipper should be of one piece construction with no seams, overlaps, rivets or sharp corners.

### *Sample bottles*

Sample bottles used for storage and transportation of milk sample should be made of good quality glass and should be suitable for sterilization. It should be wide-mouthed with glass stopper for bacteriological examination and well fitting cap or bark cork for milk meant for chemical analysis.

### *Sampling tube*

It is a straight seamless metal tube about 600 mm long of 6 mm diameter and about 1.6 mm thickness used in sampling.

### 1.1.3 Preparation of equipment for sampling

For collection of samples for chemical examination, the equipment should be clean and dry. For bacteriological examination, the equipment should be clean and sterilized. Sterilization can be done by exposing the equipment to hot air at 160°C for a minimum of 2 hours in a hot air oven or by exposing to steam at 121°C for 15-20 minutes in an autoclave. The sterile equipment can be stored for long periods for subsequent use. Another method of heat treatment includes exposure to steam at 100°C for 1 hour. Such equipment should be used on the same day. Under field conditions, it is recommended to treat the equipments by immersing them in boiling water for 5-10 minutes. Such treated material should be used immediately and cannot be stored for use at a later stage. Flaming is another method of instant sterilization. It consists of immersion in 70% ethanol and flaming to burn off the ethanol immediately before use. An appropriate method of heat treatment should be chosen keeping in view the nature, shape and size of the equipment and the conditions of sampling.

### 1.1.4 Sample collection procedures

***Sampling from milk container***

Prior to collecting the sample from an individual milk container, it is very important to thoroughly mix the milk in the container. In big containers, it can be done by stirring the milk with a long handled plunger. If the container is small, the milk can be mixed by pouring it back and forth from one vessel to another or simply by shaking it gently. Mixing will ensure that the sample is a true representative of the milk in the container.

After proper mixing, sample is drawn with sampling dipper (100-250 ml) and poured into a sample container. For bacteriological examination, the sample should be collected under aseptic conditions taking all necessary precautions to avoid any contamination. It requires the use of sterile equipments and containers. The sample bottle should be sealed and labeled.

***Sampling from different containers (Composite sample)***

When the milk is presented in several containers for sampling it is desirable to collect a composite sample from these so as to avoid analysis of large number of individual samples and, thus, saving labour and time.

A suitable method of drawing a composite sample involves pooling of the milk from all containers in a vat and subsequent mixing. From this pooled milk a sample can be drawn. If it is not possible to pool the milk, the composite sample is prepared in the following manner from the containers after milk has been agitated and mixed. First, the milk in different containers is redistributed in equal volume in a number of containers. After mixing, equal quantity of milk is taken from each container and pooled in a big vessel. A sample is collected after thorough mixing of the pooled milk. Alternatively, samples of milk may be drawn in proportion to the volumes of milk in each container. These samples are mixed in a vessel and the final sample is drawn from it.

### *Sampling bulk units*

When milk of uniform quality is supplied in bulk units (e.g. cans filled from storage tanks), random units are sampled as given below and then samples are taken from the selected units.

| Total number of units | Number of units to be selected |
|---|---|
| 1 | 1 |
| 2-5 | 2 |
| 6-20 | 3 |
| 21-60 | 4 |
| 61-100 | 5 |
| Over 100 | 5 + one for each additional 100 units or fraction thereof |

### *Sampling from storage tanks and milk tankers*

The milk in storage tanks or tankers requires very careful mixing because the volume of milk is very large. Mixing can be done using large plungers. Mechanical agitators or compressed air may also be used for this purpose. Sample should be collected after thorough mixing.

For taking the milk sample from milk tankers, agitate the milk for at least five minutes. Use a sterile milk straw or clean, sterile dipper. Do not collect sample from the valve at the bottom of the tank. Use a sterile vial and fill about three-fourth of its capacity.

### *Sampling from individual cow/animal*

Teats of the milch animal should be properly cleaned and made dry. Cotton plugs moistened with alcohol should be used to disinfect the teat ends. Scrub thoroughly until the cotton remains clean. Cleaning of far teats should be carried out first followed by cleaning of near teats to avoid contamination of the cleaned teats. Then milking should be carried out. The first few streams of milk should be discarded before collecting the milk in the vessel. After milking, the sample is collected.

### 1.1.5 Labeling and transportation of samples to laboratory

*Labeling of the sample*

Each sample container should be sealed air tight and marked with particulars regarding the purpose of sampling, name of the supplier or other particulars of the stock, date and time of sampling, the nature of preservatives added, if any, and any other related information. The purpose of sampling should also be mentioned

*Sample transport*

Milk samples should be placed on ice in an ice box immediately for transport to the laboratory. If not chilled properly, a single contaminant organism can quickly overgrow and mask the real culture result. If samples are to be shipped or held for over 24 hours, they should be frozen (unless being tested for microbiological quality) and thawed at the laboratory.

## 1.2 Rapid quality evaluation tests

### 1.2.1 Organoleptic test and visual examination

The purpose of organoleptic and visual examination of milk is to examine the sample rapidly so that apparently poor and unsatisfactory samples are identified immediately at the milk receiving platform. The test helps in detecting unsanitary conditions at the dairy farm and any apparent abnormality in milk. The test comprises of physical examination by an experienced person for any abnormal smell or colour in the milk. It can be conducted within no time.

For detection of any abnormal smell or flavour, open the container and smell the lid immediately. Observe for any abnormal or foul smell or flavour due to high acidity, feed, unclean atmosphere of the dairy farm, extraneous matter and reaction of milk with metal of the container.

For visual inspection, observe the colour of the milk. Buffalo milk is pure white while cow milk may be slightly yellowish. Record any abnormality in colour. Similarly, observe the consistency or presence of any flakes, curd particles or viscous material and record any abnormality. Physical examination also includes observing for the presence of visible dirt or particulate matter in milk.

Any milk with abnormal smell or colour should be rejected. Sometimes, the abnormality in flavour may not be clearly appreciable due to low temperature of milk. Warming of the milk improves the results. In case of doubt, the milk should be kept separate and sent for detailed examination.

### 1.2.2 pH test

It is a very rapid test mainly used for detection of abnormality in milk due to mastitis or souring of the milk due to faulty storage. It takes only few minutes.

Normal pH values of cow and buffalo milk range between 6.6 and 6.8. The milk from animals suffering from mastitis is generally alkaline in reaction and the pH in such cases may generally be above 7.0. On the other hand, any increase in acidity in milk due to bacterial multiplication leads to fall in pH. Thus, any change in pH in milk indicates abnormality in milk.

To measure the pH, take about 50 ml of milk sample in a clean beaker and measure the pH by using indicator paper strip or preferably pH meter.

### 1.2.3 Clot-on-boiling test

It is a very quick and easy test to assess the acidity in milk and thus assists in determining the suitability of milk for processing. The test is based on the fact that high acidity in milk results in its coagulation.

To perform this test, take 5 ml of milk sample in a test tube. Place the tube in a boiling water bath for 5 minutes. Then, remove the tube and rotate it gently in a slanted position and examine the walls of the test tube for any precipitated particles. The milk may also be examined for any acidic flavour.

Presence of precipitated particles on the side of the test tube and clotting/coagulation of milk is recorded as a positive test. No change in the milk is recorded as a negative test. Presence of acidic flavour, if any, is also recorded.

A positive test is considered to indicate high acidity in milk. Acidic flavour also indicates high acidity in the sample. Such milk is not suitable for distribution or processing as it will curdle on heating.

### 1.2.4 Alcohol test

Alcohol test is a rapid test which helps in the assessment of stability of milk and thus its suitability for processing. The test indicates about the mineral balance of milk and helps in detecting any abnormal milk such as colostrum, milk from animals in late lactation, milk from animals suffering from mastitis and milk with disturbed mineral balance.

The test involves mixing of 5 ml of milk sample in a test tube with 5 ml of ethyl alcohol (68% by weight or 75% by volume). It is then examined for the presence of any flakes or clot which indicates a positive test. A positive test indicates low heat stability of milk. It may also indicate high acidity in milk. Such milk is not suitable for heat processing as it will curdle on heating.

### 1.2.5 Acidity test

The test assists in measuring the acidity in milk since high acidity reduces the keeping quality and heat stability of milk. High acidity also reflects improper milk holding temperature allowing the propagation of bacteria in milk.

In this test, 20 ml of milk is titrated against a 0.1N standard sodium hydroxide solution in the presence of phenolphthalein indicator. End point is observed as development of faint pink colour that persists for one minute. The volume of NaOH solution used is noted and acidity in milk is calculated as per cent lactic acid by the following formula.

$$\text{Titrable acidity (as \% lactic acid)} = \frac{0.009 \times \text{Volume of alkali used} \times 100}{\text{Volume of milk}}$$

The increase in acidity is considered to be due to production of lactic acid as a result of propagation of contaminating bacteria in milk after its production. The normal range of apparent acidity in milk due to its natural composition is from 0.1 to 0.17 per cent. Any increase beyond 0.17% is considered as developed lactic acid (i.e. true acidity) due to bacterial growth. It indicates that milk is stale.

**Record sheet - Rapid quality evaluation tests**

| Sample details | Parameter | Observations | Interpretation |
|---|---|---|---|
| | Colour | | |
| | Flavour | | |
| | Consistency | | |
| | Particulate matter | | |
| | pH | | |
| | Clot-on-boiling test | | |
| | Alcohol test | | |
| | Acidity test | | |

| | | | |
|---|---|---|---|
| | Colour | | |
| | Flavour | | |
| | Consistency | | |
| | Particulate matter | | |
| | pH | | |
| | Clot-on-boiling test | | |
| | Alcohol test | | |
| | Acidity test | | |
| | Colour | | |
| | Flavour | | |
| | Consistency | | |
| | Particulate matter | | |
| | pH | | |
| | Clot-on-boiling test | | |
| | Alcohol test | | |
| | Acidity test | | |
| | Colour | | |
| | Flavour | | |
| | Consistency | | |
| | Particulate matter | | |
| | pH | | |

| | | | |
|---|---|---|---|
| | Clot-on-boiling test | | |
| | Alcohol test | | |
| | Acidity test | | |

Module 2

# Grading of milk by dye reduction tests

The length of time required for certain reducible dyes to change in colour when added to milk affords a simple, quick and economical method of differentiating good and poor milk. The test is an indirect method to assess the bacterial content (count) of milk.

The bacteria present in milk, when allowed to propagate, lower down the oxidation reduction potential in milk. This can be detected through the use of suitable dyes such as methylene bluc and resazurin. Addition of solution of these dyes imparts blue colour to milk. The colour fades as the dye is converted into colourless reduced compound. Thus, methylene blue is reduced to leucomethylene blue which is colourless. Resazurin is reduced to pink coloured resorufin and thereafter colourless dihydroresorufin. The time taken for discolouration depends upon the initial number of microorganisms in the milk. Higher is the bacterial count, shorter will be the reduction time. Thus, the reduction time is an indirect measure of the initial bacterial count in the sample. These tests give indication about the sanitary and keeping quality of milk and help in grading the raw milk supplies.

## 2.1 Methylene blue reduction test (Time required: 5 h 30 min)

### 2.1.1 Apparatus

Sterile test tubes with caps or stoppers (20 ml)

Sterile pipettes (1 ml,10 ml)

Test tube stand

Clock/watch

Water bath at 37 ± 0.5➡C Bunsen burner

Marking pen

### 2.1.2 Reagent

**Sterile methylene blue solution**

Dissolve a standard tablet of methylene blue thiocyanate aseptically in cold, sterile, glass-distilled water (as per the manufacturer's instructions). Store the solution in amber-glass bottle by taking aseptic precautions.

### 2.1.3 Procedure

Mix thoroughly the milk in the sample bottle.

Withdraw aseptically 10 ml of milk sample and add to the sterile screw capped test tube of 20 ml capacity.

Add 1 ml of methylene blue solution aseptically to it.

Close the tube carefully with screw cap or rubber stopper without contaminating it.

Slowly mix the contents of the tube by inverting the tube once or twice so that the whole column of the milk becomes uniform in colour.

Place the tube in a water bath maintained at 37±0.5°C temperature and note the time of beginning of the test incubation.

Observe the tubes at different intervals as described below.

### 2.1.4 Observations and recording of results

Inspect the tube for decolorization (blue to white) after 30 minutes of incubation.

A tube is considered "decolourized" when the blue colour fades away completely or upto 5 mm from the surface and the milk-dye mixture becomes white.

In case the decolourization is not observed after 30 minutes, mix the contents of the tube by gently inverting it and replace it in the water bath for further incubation.

Observe the tube again for decolourization after one hour of the first observation (i.e. total time of incubation is 1 h 30 min) and subsequently again at hourly intervals upto total 5 h 30 min till there is decolourization.

Record the time at which decolorization is observed. Methylene blue reduction time (MBRT) is recorded as 30 minutes if a sample is decolourized within 30 minutes of incubation. Thereafter, the MBRT is recorded in whole hours e.g. if the colour disappears between 30 minutes and 1 hour 30 minutes, MBRT is recorded as 1 hour and similarly if decolourization occurs between 1 hour 30 minutes and 2 hours 30 minutes, MBRT is recorded as 2 hours, and so on.

Decolourization at 5 h 30 min is recorded as MBRT 5 hours. In case of the tube showing no decolourization upto 5 h 30 min of incubation, MBRT is recorded as more than 5 hours..

### 2.1.5 Interpretation of results

The grading of raw milk samples can be done on the basis of MBRT values. The guidelines by the Bureau of Indian Standards for grading of milk are as given below.

| MBRT (hours) | Grade of raw milk |
|---|---|
| 5 and above | Very good |
| 3 and 4 | Good |
| 1 and 2 | Fair |
| ½ | Poor |

In case of pasteurized milk, MBRT should be more than 4 hours for satisfactory quality.

### 2.1.6 Precautions

Methylene blue solution should be protected from any contamination. The reagent should be stored in dark when not in use to protect from light.

Fresh reagent should be prepared frequently.

Water bath should be covered to maintain darkness inside the chamber during incubation of the tubes.

The temperature of the water bath should be brought to 37°C before beginning the test.

There should be no electric failure and the temperature of the water bath should be maintained at 37➡C throughout the period of incubation of tubes.

### 2.1.7 Limitations

The test though grades the sample on the basis of bacterial content, it does not reveal the bacterial count in the sample.

The rate of reduction of dye may vary depending upon the growth rate of different bacterial species at the given temperature.

The presence of inhibitory substances in milk may inhibit the growth of bacteria, slowing down the dye reduction.

**Record sheet -** Methylene blue reduction test

| Sample No. | Time interval | Colour | MBRT | Grade | Interpretation |
|---|---|---|---|---|---|
| | 0 min | | | | |
| | 30 min | | | | |
| | 1 h 30 min | | | | |
| | 2 h 30 min | | | | |
| | 3 h 30 min | | | | |
| | 4 h 30 min | | | | |
| | 5 h 30 min | | | | |

| | | | | | |
|---|---|---|---|---|---|
| | 0 min | | | | |
| | 30 min | | | | |
| | 1 h 30 min | | | | |
| | 2 h 30 min | | | | |
| | 3 h 30 min | | | | |
| | 4 h 30 min | | | | |
| | 5 h 30 min | | | | |
| | 0 min | | | | |
| | 30 min | | | | |
| | 1 h 30 min | | | | |
| | 2 h 30 min | | | | |
| | 3 h 30 min | | | | |
| | 4 h 30 min | | | | |
| | 5 h 30 min | | | | |
| | 0 min | | | | |
| | 30 min | | | | |
| | 1 h 30 min | | | | |
| | 2 h 30 min | | | | |
| | 3 h 30 min | | | | |
| | 4 h 30 min | | | | |
| | 5 h 30 min | | | | |
| | 0 min | | | | |
| | 30 min | | | | |
| | 1 h 30 min | | | | |
| | 2 h 30 min | | | | |
| | 3 h 30 min | | | | |
| | 4 h 30 min | | | | |
| | 5 h 30 min | | | | |

## 2.2 Half-hour methylene blue reduction test (Time required: 30 min)

Half-hour methylene blue reduction test is a rapid test to assess the bacteriological quality of raw milk. It helps in evaluating the sanitary and keeping quality of raw milk and in deciding its acceptability for processing. It is an objective test which helps in differentiating poor grade milk from the milk of acceptable quality.

### 2.2.1 Apparatus

Same as given in Section 2.1.1

### 2.2.2 Reagents

Same as given in Section 2.1.2

### 2.2.3 Procedure

The procedure is same as given in Section 2.1.3 except that incubation is done only for 30 minutes. The test requires only a single observation based on which the interpretation of the quality of milk is done.

### 2.2.4 Observations and recording of results

Observe the tube(s) after 30 minutes of incubation for decolourization (blue to white) as mentioned in Section 2.1.4.

The methylene blue reduction time (MBRT) is recorded as 30 minutes or less if the decolourization is observed within 30 minutes, otherwise the test is recorded as negative.

### 2.2.5 Interpretation

According to the guidelines by the Bureau of Indian Standards, the samples which show decolourization within 30 minutes or less are not suitable for acceptance.

### 2.2.6 Precautions

As given in Section 2.1.6.

### 2.2.7 Limitations

As given in Section 2.1.7.

**Record sheet -** Half-hour methylene blue reduction test

| Sample No. | Time interval | Colour | Result | Interpretation |
|---|---|---|---|---|
| | 0 min | | | |
| | 30 min | | | |
| | 0 min | | | |
| | 30 min | | | |
| | 0 min | | | |
| | 30 min | | | |
| | 0 min | | | |
| | 30 min | | | |
| | 0 min | | | |
| | 30 min | | | |

## 2.3. One-hour resazurin test (Time required: 1 h)

The test constitutes a simple technique for evaluation of the hygienic conditions prevailing during production and storage of milk. The test is based on same principle as the methylene blue reduction test. The test evaluates the bacteriological quality of milk and thereby assists in grading raw milk. However, the grading of milk is possible in shorter duration as compared to the methylene blue reduction test. Addition of resazurin imparts bluish colour to the milk. The resazurin changes to the resorufin (pink colour) and then further to dihydroresorufin (colourless) at different stages of the dye reduction. As a result, different samples with different bacterial loads show different shades after incubation for a particular time. The developed colour is matched with a standard colour disc in a comparator to obtain the quantitative recording of this colour shade.

### 2.3.1 Apparatus

| | |
|---|---|
| Sterile test tubes with caps or stoppers (20ml) | Sterilized rubber stoppers |
| Sterile pipettes (1 ml,10 ml) | Test tube stand |
| Water bath at 37±0.5➡C | Clock or watch |
| Comparator with standard resazurin disc | Bunsen burner |
| Marking pen | |

### 2.3.2 Reagent

**Sterile resazurin solution**

Prepare solution by dissolving a standard tablet of resazurin aseptically in sterile glass-distilled water (as indicated by the manufacturer). The solution should be prepared fresh daily in amber-coloured bottle and should be stored in refrigerator when not in use.

### 2.3.3 Procedure

Mix thoroughly the milk in the sample bottle.

Withdraw aseptically 10 ml of milk from the sample bottle into the test tube.

Add 1 ml of resazurin solution aseptically to it.

Close the tube carefully with the rubber stopper without contaminating it.

Mix the contents of the tube slowly by inverting the tube once or twice so that there is uniform mixing of the dye throughout.

Place the tube in a water bath maintained at 37±0.5°C temperature and note the time of start of incubation.

Observe the tube after 1 hour of incubation as described below.

### 2.3.4 Observations and recording of results

Take out the tubes from the water bath after incubation of one hour and match the developed colour immediately with the resazurin disc in the comparator.

For comparing, place a control tube of milk without dye in the left section of the comparator and the incubated tube in the right section.

Rotate the disc in the comparator to the point where the colour of the standard disc (control tube) matches with the incubated tube. At this point record the disc number e.g. 0, 1, 2, 3, 4 and so on.

When the colour falls between two consecutive numbers, the reading should be recorded as the half value between the two values e.g. 0.5 when the reading is between 0 and 1, 1.5 when it is between 1 and 2, and so on.

### 2.3.5 Interpretation

The disc reading helps in the grading of the milk. The guidelines prescribed by the Bureau of Indian Standards for grading of raw milk are given below.

| Disc reading | Grade |
|---|---|
| 4 or higher | Good |
| 3.5 to 1 | Fair |
| 0.5 to 0 | Poor |

### 2.3.6 Precautions

Similar to the methylene blue reduction test as given in Section 2.1.6.

### 2.3.7 Limitations

Similar to the methylene blue reduction test as given in Section 2.1.7.

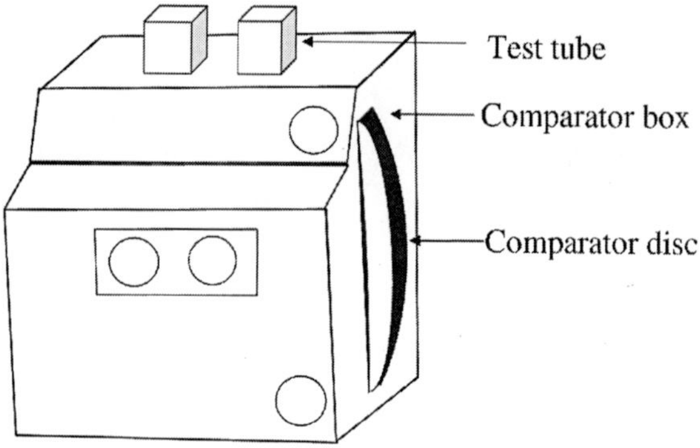


Comparator

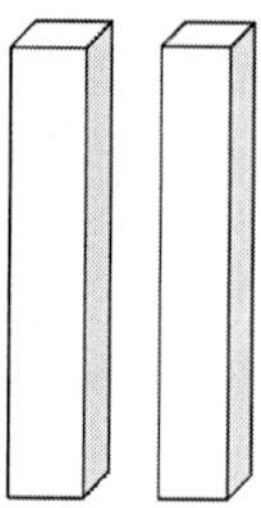

Test tubes

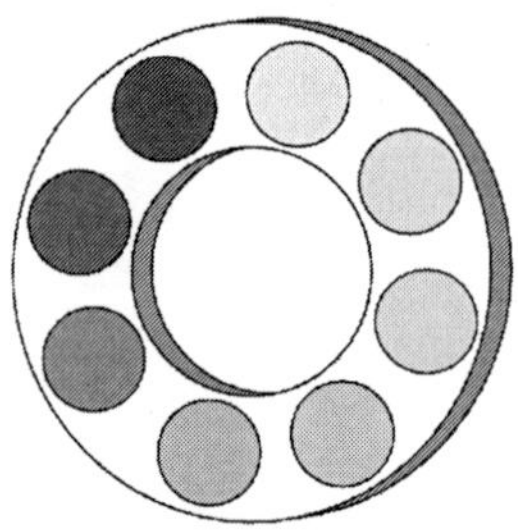

Comparator disc

**Record sheet** - Resazurin dye reduction test

| **Sample No.** | **Disc reading after 1 hour** | **Interpretation** |
|---|---|---|
| | | |
| | | |
| | | |
| | | |
| | | |

## 2.4. Ten-minutes resazurin test (Time required: 10 min)

The test is used as a platform test for detecting milk of poor keeping quality very quickly since it provides a rapid measure of sanitary condition and bacterial content of the sample. The principle of the test is same as that of resazurin dye reduction test except that incubation of the milk-dye mixture tube is done only for 10 minutes and results are recorded after 10 minutes incubation, thus, reducing time required for the test.

### 2.4.1 Apparatus

Same as given in Section 2.3.1.

### 2.4.2 Reagent

Same as given in Section 2.3.2.

### 2.4.3 Procedure

The procedure is same as given in Section 2.3.3 except that the incubation period is 10 minutes.

### 2.4.4 Observations and recording of results

Observe the tubes at the end of 10 minutes of incubation and record the results with the comparator as described in Section 2.3.4.

### 2.4.5 Interpretation

The keeping quality of milk samples is judged according to the guidelines specified by the Bureau of Indian Standards as given below.

| Disc reading | Keeping quality |
|---|---|
| 4 or higher | Satisfactory |
| 3.5 to 1 | Doubtful |
| 0.5 to 0 | Unsatisfactory |

### 2.4.6 Precautions

Similar to the methylene blue reduction test as given in Section 2.1.6.

### 2.4.7 Limitations

Similar to the methylene blue reduction test as given in Section 2.1.7.

**Record sheet -** Ten minute resazurin dye reduction test

| Sample No. | Disc reading after 10 minutes | Interpretation |
|---|---|---|
| | | |
| | | |
| | | |
| | | |
| | | |

Module 3

# Evaluation of adequacy of pasteurization of milk

It is quite important to ascertain that the milk or fluid milk products marketed as pasteurized products have been pasteurized adequately by exposing to heat at a pre-set time temperature combination sufficient to destroy all the pathogenic bacteria in the product. The following tests are used for evaluating adequacy of pasteurization:

Phosphatase test

Coliform count test

## 3.1 Phosphatase test (Time required: 2 h)

Phosphatase test is used to judge the adequacy of pasteurization of milk. It is based on the detection of phosphatase enzyme which is normally present in raw milk. This enzyme is slightly more resistant to thermal treatment than the bacterial pathogens on which validated time-temperature combinations are set for pasteurization process. Therefore, thermal inactivation of alkaline phosphatase in milk correlates well with thermal destruction of pathogenic bacteria. In case of insufficient heat treatment (i.e. less than that set for pasteurization process), some of the phosphatase enzyme remains active. The presence of enzyme in pasteurized milk indicates inadequate heat treatment or contamination of pasteurized milk with raw milk. The presence of phosphatase enzyme is detected by its action on disodium p-nitrophenyl phosphate liberating p-nitrophenyl which is yellow in alkaline solution. The intensity of the colour is compared with a blank negative control (without phosphate). A comparator is used to assess the colour intensity in quantitative terms.

### 3.1.1 Apparatus

Comparator with standard discs

Glass cells for comparator

Rubber-stoppered test tubes

Waterbath

### 3.1.2 Reagents

#### (a) Buffer solution

Dissolve 3.5 g of sodium carbonate and 1.5 g of sodium bicarbonate (analytical grade reagents) in one litre of distilled water.

#### (b) Disodium p-nitrophenyl phosphate buffer substrate

Dissolve 0.15 g of the substrate in 100 ml buffer solution (explained above) in a stoppered flask.

### 3.1.3 Procedure

Divide the milk sample in two portions, one is used for test and the other for preparing negative control.

Boil the milk meant for preparing negative control so that its phosphatase enzyme is inactivated.

Take two rubber stoppered test tubes (15 ml capacity) and label them as ‘test’ and ‘control’.

Add 10 ml buffer substrate in each of these test tubes.

Add 2 ml of test milk to the test tube labeled as ‘test’. Add 2 ml of boiled milk to the test tube labeled as ‘control’.

Incubate both the test tubes at 37°C in a water bath for 30 minutes.

After 30 minutes, transfer the contents of these tubes into the comparator cells for comparison and record the results.

Return the tubes to the water bath for incubation for further 90 minutes.

Take the second reading with comparator after incubation.

### 3.1.4 Observations and recording of results

Compare the yellow colour developed in the test sample tube with that in the control tube with comparator.

Record the disc reading where the colours of the two tubes match.

### 3.1.5 Interpretation

According to the Bureau of Indian Standards, the interpretation of the results is done as given below.

| **Disc reading after 30 minutes** | **Interpretation** |
|---|---|
| 0 or trace | properly pasteurized |
| 6 | doubtful |
| 10 or over | under pasteurized |
| **Disc reading after 2 hours** | **Interpretation** |
| 0 to 10 | properly pasteurized |
| Over 10 | under pasteurized |

Grossly inadequate pasteurization can be revealed by the reading after 30 minutes but minor error in the pasteurization can be detected on the second reading after 2 hours incubation.

### 3.1.6 Precautions

Phosphatase test should preferably be conducted immediately after pasteurization or maximum 48 hours of pasteurization, when stored at refrigeration temperature.

High quality analytic grade reagents should be used.

Buffer substrate solution should be fresh and colourless.

Rubber stoppers should be boiled before use to make them phenol-free.

Glassware should be clean and phenol-free.

It is essential to take second reading where the test is negative after 30 minutes.

### 3.1.7 Limitation

The test may be false-positive if the pasteurized milk is tested after 48 hours of pasteurization due to regeneration of phosphatase.

**Record sheet** - Phophatase test

| Sample No. | Time of reading | Disc reading | Interpretation |
|---|---|---|---|
| | 30 minutes | | |
| | 2 hours | | |
| | 30 minutes | | |
| | 2 hours | | |
| | 30 minutes | | |
| | 2 hours | | |
| | 30 minutes | | |
| | 2 hours | | |
| | 30 minutes | | |
| | 2 hours | | |

## 3.2 Coliform count test (Time required: 24 h)

While phosphatase test is a chemical test, coliform count test is a bacteriological test for determination of adequacy of pasteurization. Coliform bacteria that generally originate from intestinal tract and faecal matter are normally present in some numbers in raw milk. These bacteria are sensitive to pasteurization process. Their absence in a pasteurized milk product indicates adequacy of the pasteurization process.

For detailed procedure, please refer to Module 4, Section 4.5.

Module 4

# Microbiological examination of raw and pasteurized milk

Milk obtained from the udder of a healthy cow is expected to be very low in bacterial numbers, however, the microbiological quality of milk may deteriorate due to several factors. Bacteria gain entry to milk due to unhygienic milking methods, inadequate cleaning of equipments and in some cases, as a result of mastitis. Milk is an excellent growth medium for microorganisms when suitable temperature exists. Therefore, once bacteria enter the milk, there count increases with time, thereby resulting in reduced product quality and safety. Common tests employed for bacteriological evaluation of raw milk include direct microscopic examination, standard plate count, coliform count, psychrotrophic and thermophilic bacteria count etc. Although pasteurization kills pathogenic bacteria in milk, many types of heat resistant (thermoduric) bacteria may survive pasteurization, limiting the shelf life of pasteurized milk. Thus, routine evaluation of bacteriological quality of pasteurized milk is also important.

## 4.1 Direct microscopic examination of milk (Time required: 10-15 min)

Direct microscopic examination is a quite rapid method to determine the bacterial content of milk. It helps in grading the milk samples according to bacteriological quality. The test is quantitative and involves preparation of a smear of a measured volume of milk sample over a specified area on a glass slide, followed by staining and microscopic examination to count the number of bacteria. The morphology of contaminating bacteria can also be viewed.

### 4.1.1 Apparatus

| | |
|---|---|
| Microscope | Glass slides (marked with 1 $cm^2$ area) |
| Sterile 0.01 ml pipettes or syringes | Inoculation loop |
| Staining jar | Forceps |
| Stage micrometer | Beaker with tap water |
| Marking pen or pencil | Bunsen burner |

### 4.1.2 Reagents

#### (a) Newman's stain

This is prepared by dissolving 1 g methylene blue chloride in 100 ml of a mixture containing 54 ml of 95% ethyl alcohol, 40 ml of tetrachlorethane and 6 ml of glacial acetic acid.

#### (b) Cedar wood oil (Immersion oil)

### 4.1.3 Procedure

Take a glass slide demarcated on one side with 1cm x 1cm square area.

Clean the slide and make it grease free by gentle warming.

Gently shake the sample container for through mixing of milk and then transfer 0.01 ml of milk sample to the middle of the marked square area of glass slide on the reverse of the marked side.

Spread the sample uniformly over the marked area with a sterile inoculation loop.

Allow the smear to air dry.

Fix the smear by gentle warming without rapid and excessive heating.

Stain the slide in a staining jar containing Newman's stain for ½ to 1 minute. Take out the slide and remove excess stain by draining and then wash it gently with tap water in a beaker by changing the water thrice.

Air dry the slide, put a drop of cedar wood oil over the smear (on the smear side) and examine it under the oil-immersion objective of the microscope.

### 4.1.4 Observations and recording of results

During microscopic examination, bacterial clumps are observed which appear as groups of bacteria (single cell, in pairs, small bunch of similar cells or a large clump of similar cells).

Count the number of clumps in a certain number of microscopic fields in a systemic manner as explained in next steps.

Focus the microscope in the middle of the left vertical side of the square.

Move the slide slowly to switch over to the next microscopic field from left to right side.

Count the number of clumps in every third successive field, leaving the first two fields without counting. Counting is done in 15 microscopic fields horizontally.

Now focus the microscope in the middle of the upper line of the square and move downwards, counting clumps in 15 fields as done horizontally.

In a given microscopic field, count the number of bacterial clumps present and record the clump count in each field.

The number of microscopic fields to be counted will depend upon the bacteriological quality of the sample i.e.

average number of clumps per field. Higher is the clump count, fewer number of fields may be sufficient to interpret the results.

Usually 50, 25, 10 and 5 fields respectively, should be examined if the average clump count is 0.5, 0.5 to 1, 1 to 10 and 10 to 30, respectively. If the clump count exceeds 30 per field, the number is recorded as uncountable.

Direct microscopic clump count per ml is obtained by calculating the average number of clumps and by multiplying it with the microscopic factor.

Observe the leucocyte cells also in the microscopic fields and record them separately.

The microscopic factor can be determined by measuring the diameter of a microscopic field using stage micrometer and then applying the following formula:

$$\text{Microscopic factor} = \frac{10000}{3.1416 \times r^2}$$

where r is the radius (in mm) of the microscopic field.

The microscopic factor, once calculated for a given microscope with a definite combination of objective and ocular-piece, can be used as a constant factor.

### 4.1.5 Interpretation

The following guidelines of the Bureau of Indian Standards can be used to grade the milk sample on the basis of clump count per ml.

| Clump count per ml | Bacteriological quality |
|---|---|
| Less than 500,000 | Good |
| 500,001 to 4,000,000 | Fair |
| 4,000,001 to 20,000,000 | Poor |
| Over 20,000,000 | Very poor |

Large number of leucocyte cells (generally exceeding 500,000 per ml) together with long chains of cocci may indicate milk from the animals suffering from mastitis.

### 4.1.6 Precautions

Exactly 0.01 ml of milk sample should be delivered on the glass slide. Dropping of extra milk associated with the exterior of the pipette should be carefully prevented otherwise the results may be grossly incorrect.

The stained slide should not be washed under the running water as the smear may get washed away.

Sufficient number of fields should be examined for clumps or cells, otherwise the results may not be reliable.

While recording results, the microscopic fields showing no clump should also be recorded as zero cell or clump.

Microscopic factor should be carefully determined and the factor for one microscope should not be used for another microscope.

### 4.1.7 Limitations

The test requires skill and practice for correct results.

The accuracy of results is more in the samples with high bacterial count.

## Illustration

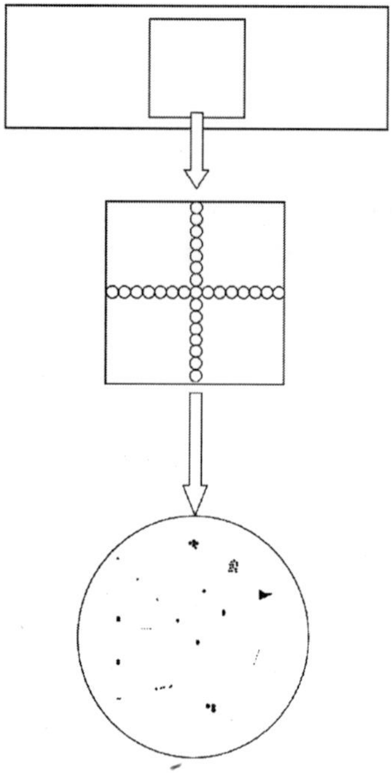

Microscopic slide with marked area of size $1cm^2$

Schematic of examining microscopic fields

Microscopic field showing bacterial clumps

**Record sheet** - Direct microscopic examination of milk

Microscopic factor of given microscope =

| Microscopic field No. | Bacterial clump count | | | | |
|---|---|---|---|---|---|
| | Sample 1 | Sample 2 | Sample 3 | Sample 4 | Sample 5 |
| | | | | | |
| | | | | | |
| | | | | | |
| | | | | | |
| | | | | | |
| | | | | | |

| | | | | | |
|---|---|---|---|---|---|
| | | | | | |
| | | | | | |
| | | | | | |
| | | | | | |
| | | | | | |
| | | | | | |
| | | | | | |
| | | | | | |
| | | | | | |
| | | | | | |
| | | | | | |
| | | | | | |
| | | | | | |
| | | | | | |
| | | | | | |
| | | | | | |
| Average clump count per field | | | | | |
| Clump count per ml | | | | | |
| Bacteriological quality/ Grade | | | | | |
| Bacterial morphology | | | | | |
| Leucocyte cells | | | | | |
| Interpretation | | | | | |

## 4.2 Standard plate count test (Time required: 24-48 h)

The standard plate count (SPC) test is useful in assessing the number of viable bacteria in milk. The count helps to grade the milk into different categories. In heat-processed milk, the test indicates the number of bacteria surviving the heat treatment and thus reflects the keeping quality. The number of colony forming units (cfu) of bacteria obtained on a culture medium plate multiplied by the dilution factor gives SPC per ml of milk.

### 4.2.1 Apparatus

| | |
|---|---|
| Sterilized petri dishes | 1 ml pipettes |
| Test tubes | Test tube rack |
| Water bath preset at 45°C | Incubator or BOD incubator |
| Burner | Marking pen |

### 4.2.2 Culture medium/reagents

**(a) Plate count agar:** Prepare the medium according to the composition given below.

| | | |
|---|---|---|
| Pancreatic digest of casein | : | 5 g |
| Yeast extract | : | 2.5 g |
| Dextrose | : | 1 g |
| Agar agar | : | 15 g |

Suspend all the ingredients in 1 liter distilled water, heat to boil to dissolve and then autoclave at 121°C for 15 minutes.

**(b) Normal saline solution (NSS)**

Dissolve 0.85 g of sodium chloride in 1 liter of distilled water and autoclave to sterilize. Dispense 9 ml solution in test tubes aseptically.

### 4.2.3 Procedure

Take 9 ml sterile NSS aseptically in six sterile test tubes and mark these tubes as 1:10, 1:100, 1:1000 ($10^{-1}$, $10^{-2}$, and $10^{-3}$) and so on for making serial decimal dilutions of the milk sample.

Take a sterile pipette and aseptically transfer 1 ml of the sample after thorough mixing to the 1:10 test tube. Discard the pipette.

Take another sterile pipette and mix the contents of 1:10 test tube and then transfer 1 ml from this to the next tube 1:100.

Make further serial dilutions in the same fashion upto $10^{-6}$ using fresh pipette each time and without touching the NSS or wall of the test tube with the tip of the pipette.

Number of dilutions can be reduced in case of heat processed milk samples which are expected to carry less bacterial load. Similarly, the number of serial dilutions should be increased in case of samples expected to carry higher bacterial load.

Now take two sterile petri dishes for each dilution and mark the sample number, dilution, date etc. on the bottom.

Take a fresh sterile pipette and after thorough mixing inoculate 1 ml of $10^{-6}$ dilution (or the highest dilution) of the sample in each of the two petri dishes corresponding to that dilution.

Transfer lower dilutions ($10^{-5}$, $10^{-4}$, $10^{-3}$ and so on) of the sample to the corresponding petri dishes in a similar way. The same pipette can be used if inoculation is done beginning with the highest dilution and moving to the lower dilution serially.

Pour 15-20 ml (approx.) plate count agar culture medium (melted and held at 45➡C in water bath) to each petri dish and mix the sample and the culture medium by giving gentle rotation to the petri dish in a horizontal plane.

Allow the contents to solidify at room temperature.

Incubate the petri dishes in inverted position (bottom side up) in an incubator at 37°C for 24 hours or at 30°C for 48 hours.

### 4.2.4 Observations and recording of results

Observe the petri dishes for the presence of visible colonies that are present on the surface or within the media.

Select the pair of petri dishes of the dilution that reveals colonies between 30 and 300 in number. Note down the dilution

Count the number of colonies in each plate irrespective of shape and size. Record the number and find out the average number of colony forming units (cfu).

Multiply the average cfu number with the corresponding dilution factor (e.g. 10 for 1:10 dilution, 100 for 1:100 dilution, 1000 for 1:1000 dilution and so on) to obtain the SPC per ml in the sample.

### 4.2.5 Interpretation

Grading of milk can be done according to the Bureau of Indian Standards (BIS) guidelines as given below:

| Grade | SPC/ml |
|---|---|
| Very good | not exceeding $2x10^5$ |
| Good | $2x10^5$ to $1x10^6$ |
| Fair | $1x10^6$ to $5x10^6$ |
| Poor | above $5x10^6$ |

According to BIS guidelines, SPC in pasteurized milk should not exceed 30,000 per ml in the final container at dairy plant.

### 4.2.6 Precautions

The test should be performed by a trained person who is skilled in bacteriological work.

The temperature of the culture medium while pouring in the petri dishes should not be too high.

Colonies should be counted by holding the petri dish against diffused light so as to see all the colonies present at all the levels in the culture medium i.e. on the surface, subsurface or bottom.

Very minute colonies should also be taken into account.

### 4.2.7 Limitations

The test does not give the actual total viable count since many organisms may not be able to form colonies in the given culture medium or under the given environmental conditions (temperature, aerobic condition) used in the test. For example, many fastidious, psychrophilic, thermophilic or anaerobic bacteria may not form visible colonies and thus remain unaccounted.

The test requires a skilled laboratory worker.

The duration of the test is very long.

The test does not reflect the nature of bacteria i.e. whether pathogenic or non-pathogenic.

## Illustration

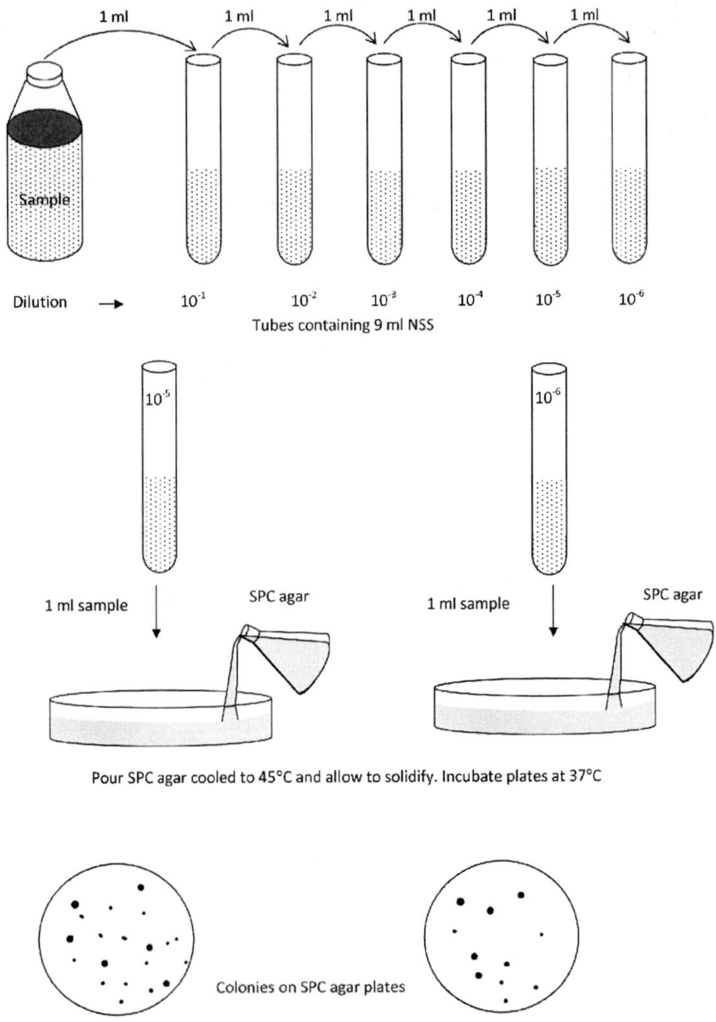

**Record sheet -** Standard plate count test

| Sample No. | Dilution | Colony count (cfu) | | | Dilution factor | SPC/ml | Grade of milk |
|---|---|---|---|---|---|---|---|
| | | Plate I | Plate II | Average | | | |
| | $10^{-1}$ | | | | $10^{1}$ | | |
| | $10^{-2}$ | | | | $10^{2}$ | | |
| | $10^{-3}$ | | | | $10^{3}$ | | |
| | $10^{-4}$ | | | | $10^{4}$ | | |
| | $10^{-5}$ | | | | $10^{5}$ | | |
| | $10^{-6}$ | | | | $10^{6}$ | | |
| | $10^{-1}$ | | | | $10^{1}$ | | |
| | $10^{-2}$ | | | | $10^{2}$ | | |
| | $10^{-3}$ | | | | $10^{3}$ | | |
| | $10^{-4}$ | | | | $10^{4}$ | | |
| | $10^{-5}$ | | | | $10^{5}$ | | |
| | $10^{-6}$ | | | | $10^{6}$ | | |
| | $10^{-1}$ | | | | $10^{1}$ | | |
| | $10^{-2}$ | | | | $10^{2}$ | | |
| | $10^{-3}$ | | | | $10^{3}$ | | |
| | $10^{-4}$ | | | | $10^{4}$ | | |
| | $10^{-5}$ | | | | $10^{5}$ | | |
| | $10^{-6}$ | | | | $10^{6}$ | | |
| | $10^{-1}$ | | | | $10^{1}$ | | |
| | $10^{-2}$ | | | | $10^{2}$ | | |
| | $10^{-3}$ | | | | $10^{3}$ | | |
| | $10^{-4}$ | | | | $10^{4}$ | | |
| | $10^{-5}$ | | | | $10^{5}$ | | |
| | $10^{-6}$ | | | | $10^{6}$ | | |

## 4.3. Psychrophilic and psychrotrophic bacteria count test (Time required: 7 days)

Psychrophilic and psychrotrophic bacteria are able to grow at low temperatures (below 10°C) and may cause spoilage of milk held at refrigeration temperatures. Enumeration of these bacteria assumes significance because of their ability to reduce the shelf life of the products even when held in refrigerators. The principle of the test is similar to the SPC test except that the petri dishes are incubated at 5-7°C for 7 days because psychrophiles and psychrotrophs are able to grow and form visible colonies at this temperature.

### 4.3.1 Apparatus

Same as in the standard plate count (SPC) test detailed in Section 4.2.1. In addition, a BOD incubator or refrigerator maintained at 5-7°C is required.

### 4.3.2 Culture medium/reagents

Same as in the SPC test detailed in Section 4.2.2.

### 4.3.3 Procedure

The procedure is similar to the SPC test (given in Section 4.2.3) except that the inoculated petri dishes are subjected to incubation at 5-7°C for 7 days.

### 4.3.4 Observations and recording of results

After completion of the incubation period, plates are observed and results are recorded by similar procedure as for the SPC test detailed in Section 4.2.4.

### 4.3.5 Interpretations

In case of raw milk, large number of psychrophilic and psychrotrophic organisms reflect the poor keeping quality at low temperature. In case of pasteurized milk, the presence of psychrophilic or psychrotropic organisms in large number may be due to post-pasteurization contamination resulting in shorter shelf life at refrigeration temperature.

### 4.3.6 Precautions

Same precautions are required as in the SPC test mentioned in Section 4.2.6.

### 4.3.7 Limitations

The test cannot differentiate between psychrotrophic and psychrophilic bacteria and gives their total count.

The incubation period is too long and results are available only after 5-7 days.

**Record sheet -** Psychrophillic and psychrotrophic bacteria count test

| Sample No. | Dilution | Colony count (cfu) | | | Dilution factor | cfu/ ml | Interpretation |
|---|---|---|---|---|---|---|---|
| | | Plate I | Plate II | Average | | | |
| | $10^{-1}$ | | | | $10^{1}$ | | |
| | $10^{-2}$ | | | | $10^{2}$ | | |
| | $10^{-3}$ | | | | $10^{3}$ | | |
| | $10^{-4}$ | | | | $10^{4}$ | | |
| | $10^{-5}$ | | | | $10^{5}$ | | |
| | $10^{-6}$ | | | | $10^{6}$ | | |
| | $10^{-1}$ | | | | $10^{1}$ | | |
| | $10^{-2}$ | | | | $10^{2}$ | | |
| | $10^{-3}$ | | | | $10^{3}$ | | |
| | $10^{-4}$ | | | | $10^{4}$ | | |
| | $10^{-5}$ | | | | $10^{5}$ | | |
| | $10^{-6}$ | | | | $10^{6}$ | | |

| | $10^{-1}$ | | | | $10^{1}$ | | |
|---|---|---|---|---|---|---|---|
| | $10^{-2}$ | | | | $10^{2}$ | | |
| | $10^{-3}$ | | | | $10^{3}$ | | |
| | $10^{-4}$ | | | | $10^{4}$ | | |
| | $10^{-5}$ | | | | $10^{5}$ | | |
| | $10^{-6}$ | | | | $10^{6}$ | | |
| | $10^{-1}$ | | | | $10^{1}$ | | |
| | $10^{-2}$ | | | | $10^{2}$ | | |
| | $10^{-3}$ | | | | $10^{3}$ | | |
| | $10^{-4}$ | | | | $10^{4}$ | | |
| | $10^{-5}$ | | | | $10^{5}$ | | |
| | $10^{-6}$ | | | | $10^{6}$ | | |
| | $10^{-1}$ | | | | $10^{1}$ | | |
| | $10^{-2}$ | | | | $10^{2}$ | | |
| | $10^{-3}$ | | | | $10^{3}$ | | |
| | $10^{-4}$ | | | | $10^{4}$ | | |
| | $10^{-5}$ | | | | $10^{5}$ | | |
| | $10^{-6}$ | | | | $10^{6}$ | | |

## 4.4. Thermophilic bacteria count test (Time required: 2 days)

Thermophilic bacteria are able to grow at temperatures above 45°C with optimum growth at 55-65°C. The test gives estimate of thermophilic bacteria in milk. High thermophilic count reflects unhygienic conditions during production and handling of milk. The principle of the test is similar to the SPC test except that the thermophilic bacteria form visible colonies at 55°C in a period of 2 days.

### 4.4.1 Apparatus

Same as in the standard plate count (SPC) test detailed in Section 4.2.1.

### 4.4.2 Culture medium/reagents

Same as in the SPC test detailed in Section 4.2.2.

### 4.4.3 Procedure

The procedure is similar to the SPC test (given in Section 4.2.3) except that the inoculated petri dishes are subjected to incubation at 55°C for 2 days.

### 4.4.4 Observations and recording of results

After completion of the incubation period, plates should be observed and results are recorded by similar procedure as for the SPC test detailed in Section 4.2.4.

### 4.4.5 Interpretations

Large number of thermophilic bacteria in raw milk indicates unhygienic practices during milk production and handling.

These bacteria may survive pasteurization process resulting in poor quality pasteurized product. These organisms may also build up in the pasteurization plant if cleaning of the plant is not efficient.

### 4.4.6 Precautions

Precautions to be taken are same as in the SPC test mentioned in Section 4.2.6.

### 4.4.7 Limitation

The test may not give actual number of thermophilic bacteria since certain bacteria (e.g. anaerobes) may not grow under the conditions provided in the test.

**Record sheet -** Thermophillic bacteria count test

| Sample No. | Dilution | Colony count (cfu) | | | Dilution factor | cfu/ml | Interpretation |
|---|---|---|---|---|---|---|---|
| | | Plate I | Plate II | Average | | | |
| | $10^{-1}$ | | | | $10^{1}$ | | |
| | $10^{-2}$ | | | | $10^{2}$ | | |
| | $10^{-3}$ | | | | $10^{3}$ | | |
| | $10^{-4}$ | | | | $10^{4}$ | | |
| | $10^{-5}$ | | | | $10^{5}$ | | |
| | $10^{-6}$ | | | | $10^{6}$ | | |
| | $10^{-1}$ | | | | $10^{1}$ | | |
| | $10^{-2}$ | | | | $10^{2}$ | | |
| | $10^{-3}$ | | | | $10^{3}$ | | |
| | $10^{-4}$ | | | | $10^{4}$ | | |
| | $10^{-5}$ | | | | $10^{5}$ | | |
| | $10^{-6}$ | | | | $10^{6}$ | | |
| | $10^{-1}$ | | | | $10^{1}$ | | |
| | $10^{-2}$ | | | | $10^{2}$ | | |
| | $10^{-3}$ | | | | $10^{3}$ | | |
| | $10^{-4}$ | | | | $10^{4}$ | | |
| | $10^{-5}$ | | | | $10^{5}$ | | |
| | $10^{-6}$ | | | | $10^{6}$ | | |
| | $10^{-1}$ | | | | $10^{1}$ | | |
| | $10^{-2}$ | | | | $10^{2}$ | | |
| | $10^{-3}$ | | | | $10^{3}$ | | |
| | $10^{-4}$ | | | | $10^{4}$ | | |
| | $10^{-5}$ | | | | $10^{5}$ | | |
| | $10^{-6}$ | | | | $10^{6}$ | | |

## 4.5 Coliform count test (Time required: 24 h)

Coliform group of bacteria comprises of *E. coli*, *Enterobacter*, *Klebsiella* and *Citrobacter*, all members of family Enterobacteriaceae. These all are lactose fermentors. Coliform organisms mainly originate from intestinal tract and faecal matter. They gain access to raw milk from the surrounding environment during production and handling of milk at dairy farm. Their presence in excessive numbers in raw milk indicates unsatisfactory hygienic practices during milk production. Coliforms are heat-sensitive and are destroyed by pasteurization of milk. Their presence in pasteurized milk, therefore, suggests either inadequate pasteurization of milk or contamination after pasteurization. The test is mainly performed to confirm the adequacy of pasteurization process and to rule out any post-pasteurization contamination, however, it may also be used to know about the hygienic practices and sanitary conditions during the production of milk and other dairy products.

Enumeration of coliforms is done by plating appropriate dilutions of the sample on violet red bile agar (VRBA), a selective culture medium. VRBA has inhibitory effect on those bacteria which, unlike coliforms, are not bile-resistant. Coliforms change sodium desoxycholate (bile salt) into desoxycholic acid which is non-soluble and precipitates out with dye and gives rise to reddish colonies surrounded by violet red zone. The diameter of the colonies of coliform bacteria after incubation for 24 hours at 37°C is 0.5 mm or more.

### 4.5.1 Apparatus

Same as in the standard plate count (SPC) test detailed in Section 4.2.1.

## Culture medium/reagents

### (a) Violet red bile agar

| | | |
|---|---|---|
| Yeast extract | : | 3 g |
| Peptone | : | 7 g |
| Bile salt No. 3 | : | 1.5 g |
| Lactose | : | 10 g |
| Sodium chloride | : | 5 g |
| Neutral red | : | 30 mg |
| Crystal violet | : | 2 mg |
| Agar agar | : | 15 g |

Suspend all the ingredients in 1 liter of distilled water. Dissolve by heating with frequent agitation and boil for 1 minute. Do not autoclave. Keep this medium in melted form at 45°C in water bath till used.

### (b) Sterilized 0.85% saline solution (NSS)

Prepare as per instructions given in Section 4.2.2.

### 4.5.3 Procedure

Prepare serial decimal dilutions of milk sample in NSS as described in the SPC test. Normally for hygienically produced raw milk, 1:100 dilution may be sufficient but higher dilutions may be required for samples suspected to carry large numbers of coliforms. For pasteurized milk, 1:10 dilution may be enough.

Inoculate 1 ml of diluted sample in duplicate petri dishes as described in the SPC test.

Pour 15-20 ml of VRBA culture medium in each plate, mix and allow to solidify.

After solidification of the medium, pour another thin layer of VRBA (3-4 ml) to cover the entire surface of the previously solidified medium. Allow to solidify.

Incubate at 37°C for 24 hours.

### 4.5.4 Observations and recording of results

Observe the plates for the presence of characteristic colonies of coliform bacteria in appropriate dilution.

Calculate coliform count per ml by multiplying the average colony count in the selected pair of petri dishes with the corresponding dilution factor.

### 4.5.5 Interpretation

According to the Bureau of Indian Standards, raw milk may be considered satisfactory if coliforms are absent in 1:100 dilution. Excessive coliform count indicates unhygienic conditions during milk production.

In case of pasteurized milk, coliform bacteria should be absent in 1:10 dilution of the sample. The presence of coliform indicates inadequate pasteurization or post-pasteurization contamination.

### 4.5.6 Precautions

VRBA medium once solidified gets spoiled if boiled for melting again. Therefore, the medium after melting should be kept in a water bath at 45-48°C till used.

A covering layer of VRBA is necessary, otherwise the colonies formed on the surface may be large and without characteristic colour.

Overcrowding of colonies in a petri dish should be avoided by using next higher dilution, otherwise the size of the colonies may not reach the characteristic 0.5 mm.

### 4.5.7 Limitation

Coliform test though detects faulty pasteurization process but cannot differentiate between inadequate pasteurization and post-pasteurization contamination.

## Illustration

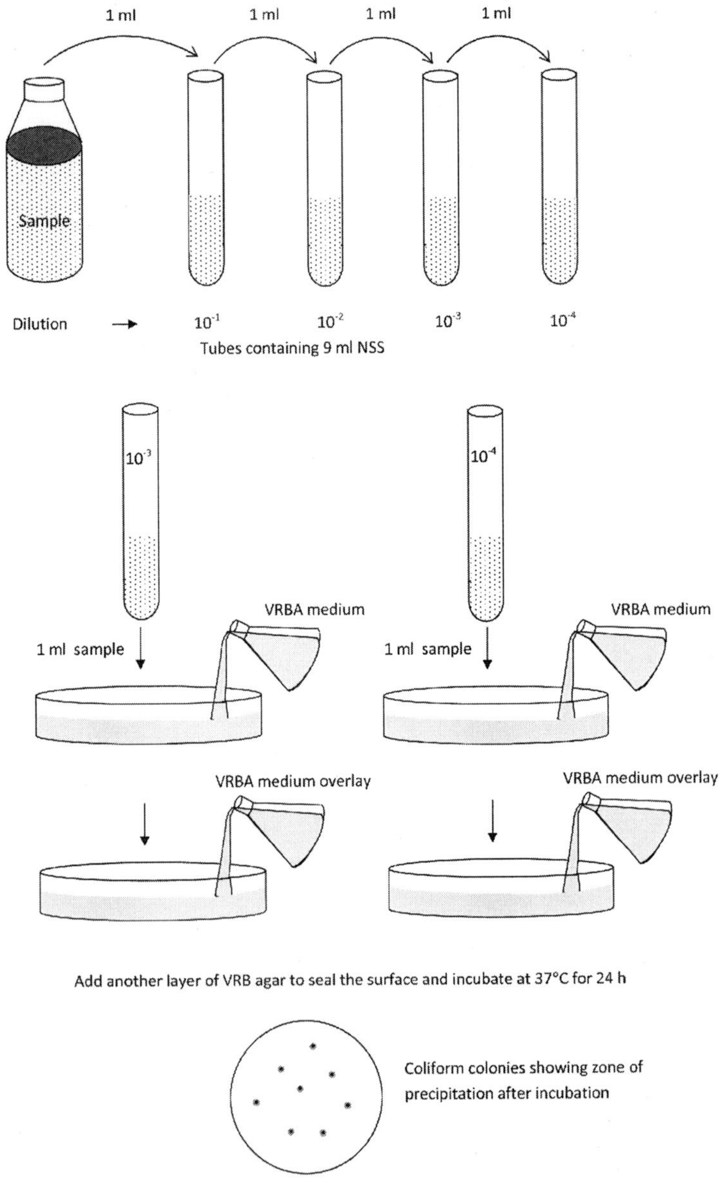

**Record sheet** - Coliform count test

| Sample No. | Dilution | Coliform colony count | | | Dilution factor | Coliforms/ ml | Interpretation |
|---|---|---|---|---|---|---|---|
| | | Plate I | Plate II | Average | | | |
| | $10^{-1}$ | | | | $10^{1}$ | | |
| | $10^{-2}$ | | | | $10^{2}$ | | |
| | $10^{-3}$ | | | | $10^{3}$ | | |
| | $10^{-4}$ | | | | $10^{4}$ | | |
| | $10^{-5}$ | | | | $10^{5}$ | | |
| | $10^{-6}$ | | | | $10^{6}$ | | |
| | $10^{-1}$ | | | | $10^{1}$ | | |
| | $10^{-2}$ | | | | $10^{2}$ | | |
| | $10^{-3}$ | | | | $10^{3}$ | | |
| | $10^{-4}$ | | | | $10^{4}$ | | |
| | $10^{-5}$ | | | | $10^{5}$ | | |
| | $10^{-6}$ | | | | $10^{6}$ | | |
| | $10^{-1}$ | | | | $10^{1}$ | | |
| | $10^{-2}$ | | | | $10^{2}$ | | |
| | $10^{-3}$ | | | | $10^{3}$ | | |
| | $10^{-4}$ | | | | $10^{4}$ | | |
| | $10^{-5}$ | | | | $10^{5}$ | | |
| | $10^{-6}$ | | | | $10^{6}$ | | |
| | $10^{-1}$ | | | | $10^{1}$ | | |
| | $10^{-2}$ | | | | $10^{2}$ | | |
| | $10^{-3}$ | | | | $10^{3}$ | | |
| | $10^{-4}$ | | | | $10^{4}$ | | |
| | $10^{-5}$ | | | | $10^{5}$ | | |
| | $10^{-6}$ | | | | $10^{6}$ | | |
| | $10^{-1}$ | | | | $10^{1}$ | | |
| | $10^{-2}$ | | | | $10^{2}$ | | |
| | $10^{-3}$ | | | | $10^{3}$ | | |
| | $10^{-4}$ | | | | $10^{4}$ | | |
| | $10^{-5}$ | | | | $10^{5}$ | | |
| | $10^{-6}$ | | | | $10^{6}$ | | |

Module 5

# Microbiological examination of milk products

Besides fresh milk, a variety of milk products are available to the consumers. These products are normally heat processed and produced on large scale in dairy plants, however, some products may also be prepared in small scale cottage industries. Common heat processed fluid products include pasteurized milk, sterilized milk and flavoured milk. Other dairy products which are solid, semisolid or of thicker consistency include cream, butter, ice cream, condensed milk, milk powder, infant milk foods, processed cheese and fermented products such as curd and yoghurt. Besides these, there are certain very popular indigenous products like khoa, burfi, paneer, kulfi, chakka, shrikhand and canned rasogulla etc. Whether fluid or solid, these are generally ready to eat food items, due to which their hygienic quality and safety assurance assumes greater importance.

The tests for evaluation of hygienic quality of these products mainly include standard plate count (SPC), coliform count, psychrotrophic bacteria count, yeast and mould count and tests for pathogens. Phosphatase test is also done in case of heat processed products.

The principles and methods of these tests are largely similar to those described for milk in the foregoing Modules. Some modifications in the methodology are required while analyzing dairy products that are solid or thick in consistency.

## 5.1 Collection, storage, transport and preparation of samples

### 5.1.1 Sampling of fluid milk and fluid dairy products

The samples of fluid products are collected after through mixing of the product in the container. For microbiological analysis, the samples should be collected aseptically in sterile containers using presterilized equipments such as plungers and sampling dippers.

### 5.1.2 Sampling of solid dairy products

The mixing and homogenization of solid food products is not as feasible as in the liquid products. However, care should be taken to collect the sample in such a way that it is true representative of the product. Aseptic precautions should be carefully observed while collecting specimens for microbiological analysis.

Samples of retail packages of products such as milk powder, condensed milk, baby food, butter, ice cream etc. should be collected in a systematic manner. Adequate number of unopened containers based upon the size of the total lot should be collected and sent to the laboratory.

In case of bulk packages, representative portions from the middle and all corners of the lot should be collected and pooled. Sterile spoons or spatula can be used to draw samples from different portions of the products like butter, ice cream and ghee etc.

For collection of surface samples of the products like cheese, samples should be collected with the help of a spatula or cutter.

### 5.1.3 Storage and transport of samples

The samples should be transported to the laboratory as quickly as possible, preferably within 24 hours of collection. If any delay is anticipated, the samples should be stored at 0-2➡C.

The temperature of the samples during transport should be maintained at 0-5➡C by using insulated containers or ice boxes. However, the products with long shelf life may be stored and transported at higher temperature upto 25➡C.

### 5.1.4 Preparation of samples for microbiological analysis

The procedure of diluting dairy products and the required number of serial dilutions may differ for each product. In case of solid, concentrated or cultured dairy products, the initial dilution is made by suspending 11 g of sample in 99 ml of diluent.

The samples should be minced and triturated with pestle in a mortar and homogenized in the diluent under aseptic conditions. An electric blender or homogenizer is preferable for making a uniform 1:10 suspension of the sample.

Further, serial dilutions should be prepared by transferring 1 ml of the 1:10 suspension to 9 ml of diluent.

Butter may be brought to fluid state by holding the butter sample container at 40°C in a water bath for 10-15 minutes to melt it. The bottles containing sterile diluent (0.85% saline solution) and pipettes should also be warmed to 40-45°C before attempting the dilution of the sample.

For low count products, only few or no further dilutions may be required. The detail of the tests required for some common dairy products are given below in short.

## 5.2 Heat processed fluid milk and milk products

Heat processed fluid milk and milk products include pasteurized milk, sterilized milk, flavoured milk etc.

Major tests for hygienic evaluation of these products include standard plate count (SPC), coliform count and phosphatase test.

The methods of examination are similar to those for raw milk, however, due to their heat processed nature, fewer dilutions may be required for pasteurized products and none for the sterilized products for obtaining bacterial count in these products.

The interpretation of results should be done on the basis of the standards/guidelines for a particular product. Some guidelines prescribed by the Bureau of Indian Standards for these products are noted below.

### Pasteurized milk

SPC should not exceed 30,000 per ml.

Coliform bacteria should be absent in 1:10 dilution of the sample.

Phosphatase test should be negative.

### Sterilized milk

SPC should not exceed 5 per ml.

Coliforms should be absent.

### Pasteurized flavoured milk

SPC should not exceed 50,000 per ml.

Coliform count should not exceed 10 per ml.

Phosphatase test should be negative.

## 5.3 Cream

SPC, coliform count and phosphatase tests are useful in evaluating the quality of cream.

Grading of raw cream based on SPC test can be done using guidelines of the Bureau of Indian Standards as given below.

| SPC per ml (or g) | Grade |
|---|---|
| Below 400,000 | Very good |
| 400,000 – 2,000,000 | Good |
| 2,000,000 – 10,000,000 | Fair |
| Over 10,000,000 | Poor |

In pasteurized cream, the SPC should not exceed 60,000 per ml (or g) in the dairy plant.

Coliform count should not be more than 100 per ml (or g) in raw cream and not more than 10 per ml in pasteurized cream.

Phosphatase test should be negative in pasteurized and sterilized products.

## 5.4 Butter

Common microbiological tests for butter include SPC, coliform count, psychrotrophic bacteria count and yeast and mould count.

According to the Bureau of Indian Standards, coliform count should not exceed 10 per ml in satisfactory quality butter. Higher number of coliforms indicates improper pasteurization of cream or contamination of butter during production and packaging.

Based on yeast and mould counts, the quality of butter may be graded according to the Bureau of Indian Standards guidelines as shown below.

| Yeast and mould count per ml | Grade |
|---|---|
| Below 20 | Good |
| 21-50 | Fair |
| 51-100 | Poor |
| Over 100 | Very poor |

## 5.5 Ice cream

The SPC, coliform count, psychrotrophic bacteria count, yeast and mould count and phosphatase test are the common tests performed to judge the hygienic quality of ice cream.

Bureau of Indian Standards recommends that the SPC in ice cream should not be more than 2,50,000 per g and coliform count not more than 90 per g.

Phosphatase test should be negative.

## 5.6 Condensed milk (sweetened)

It should be examined for SPC, coliform count, yeast and mould count and sterility test.

The SPC should not exceed 500 per g and yeast and mould counts should not be more than 10 per g in full-cream and skimmed condensed milk according to the Bureau of Indian Standards. The coliform test in the products should be negative.

## 5.7 Milk powder and infant milk foods

The samples of milk powder and infant milk foods should be examined for SPC, coliform count and yeast and mould count, psychrotrophic bacteria count and thermophilic bacteria count for quality evaluation. These may also be examined for pathogens, if necessary.

According to Bureau of Indian Standards, SPC should not exceed 50,000 per g in these products.

Coliform count should not be more than 90 per g in milk powder and 10 per g in infant milk foods.

## 5.8 Processed cheese

Processed cheese may be examined for SPC, coliform count, yeast and mould count and psychrotrophic bacteria count to judge the hygienic quality.

Tins are also examined by incubating at 30°C for 14 days. There should be no bulging of tins due to gas production.

## 5.9 Fermented milk products

The fermented milk products like 'dahi' and yoghurt should be examined for yeast and mould counts, coliform count and phosphatase tests.

Dahi and yoghurt should not have more than 100 per g yeast and mould count and 10 per g coliform count. Phosphatase test should be negative in these products.

## 5.10 Indigenous milk products

Indigenous products like khoa, burfi, paneer, kulfi, chakka, shrikhand and canned rasogulla can be assessed for hygienic quality by testing for SPC, coliform count and yeast and mould count.

The guidelines prescribed by the Bureau of Indian Standards for these products are given below.

| **Products** | **SPC (maximum, cfu/g)** | **Coliform count (maximum, cfu/g)** | **Yeast and mould count (maximum, cfu/g)** |
|---|---|---|---|
| Khoa | NS | 90 | 50 |
| Burfi | 30,000 | NS | 10 |
| Paneer | 5,00,000 | 100 | 250 |
| Kulfi | 2,50,000 | 100 | NS |
| Chakka | NS | 10 | 20 |
| Shrikhand | NS | 10 | 50 |
| Canned rasogulla | 500 | Nil | NS |

NS – not specified

## 5.11 Food Safety and Standards Regulations, 2011

The Food Safety and Standards Authority of India has recently notified Food Safety and Standards Regulations (2011). The microbiological requirements for different processed milk and milk products in these regulations have been summarized in Table 5.1.

The quality of milk and milk products should therefore, be evaluated accordingly.

**Table 5.1 Microbiological requirements for processed milk and milk products as per Food Safety and Standards (Food Products Standards and Food Additives) Regulations, 2011 (India)**

| Product (n=5) | Sampling plan | Total plate count | Coliform count | Yeast and mould count |
|---|---|---|---|---|
| Pasteurised milk, cream, flavoured milk | m | 30,000/g (c=2) | - | - |
| | M | 50,000/g | <10/g | - |
| Sterilized and UHT milk, cream, flavoured milk, evaporated milk | M | Nil | - | - |
| Sweetened condensed milk | m | 500/g (c=2) | - | - |
| | M | 1500/g | <10/g | 10/g |
| Pasteurised butter | m | 10,000/g (c=2) | 10/g (c=2) | 20/g (c=2) |
| | M | 50,000/g | 50/g | 50/g |
| Dried products: milk powder, cream, whey, edible casein, ice cream mix | m | 40,000/g (c=2) | 10/g (c=2) | - |
| | M | 50,000/g | 50/g | - |
| Ice cream, frozen dessert, milk lolly, ice candy | m | 2,00,000/g (c=2) | 50/g (c=2) | - |
| | M | 2,50,000/g | 100/g | <10/g |

| Product (n=5) | Sampling plan | Total plate count | Coliform count | Yeast and mould count |
|---|---|---|---|---|
| Processed cheese, cheese spread | m | 50,000/g (c=2) | - | - |
| | M | 75,000/g | <10/g | <10/g |
| All other cheeses | m | - | 100/g (c=2) | 10/g (c=2) |
| | M | - | 500/g | 100/g |
| Yoghurt, dahi, chakka, shrikhand | m | - | 10/g (c=2) | 50/g (c=2) |
| | M | - | 50/g | 100g |
| Paneer chhana | m | 3,00,000/g (c=2) | 50/g (c=2) | 150/g (c=2) |
| | M | 5,00,000/g | 90/g | 250/g |
| Khoya | m | 50,000/g (c=2) | 50/g (c=2) | 50/g (c=2) |
| | M | 1,00,000/g | 90/g | 100/g |

n = The number of sample units which must be examined from the batch/lot of food.

m = Represents an acceptable level and values above it are marginally acceptable in terms of the sampling plan.

M = A microbiological criterion which separates marginally acceptable quality from unsatisfactory/potentially hazardous quality. Values above M are unacceptable and detection of one or more samples exceeding this level would be cause for rejection of the lot.

c = The maximum allowable number of defective sample units which may exceed the microbiological limit

n = The number of sample units which must be examined from the batch/lot of food to satisfy the requirements of a particular sampling plan specified by m.

**Record sheet -** Microbiological examination of milk products

| Sample No. | Sample details | Test results | | | | Interpretation |
|---|---|---|---|---|---|---|
| | | SPC | Coliforms | Psychro-trophs | Thermo-philes | |
| | | | | | | |
| | | | | | | |
| | | | | | | |
| | | | | | | |
| | | | | | | |
| | | | | | | |
| | | | | | | |
| | | | | | | |
| | | | | | | |
| | | | | | | |

Module 6

# Detection of adulterants in milk

Adulteration of milk to derive extra profits through fraudulent means is quite common. The unscrupulous vendors may add different types of chemicals to disguise the poor quality milk as an attractive good looking product. Milk may be adulterated with starch, gelatin, cane sugar, sucrose or calcium carbonate to make the milk look more viscous and thick. Neutralizers such as sodium bicarbonate or sodium carbonate are added to mask the developed acidity in stale milk. Urea and detergent are used in making synthetic milk. Adulteration in milk can be detected by quick tests based on the chemical reaction of adulterants with diagnostic reagents.

## Apparatus

| | |
|---|---|
| Test tubes | Pipettes |
| Conical flasks | Water bath |

## Reagents

| | |
|---|---|
| 1% iodine solution | Concentrated HCl |
| Saturated picric acid aqueous solution | Mercuric nitrate solution |
| Resorcinol | Alcohol |
| 1% alcoholic solution of rosalic acid | 2% NaOH solution |
| 2% sodium hypochlorite solution | 5% phenol solution |
| 24% trichloroacetic acid (TCA) solution | 0.5% bromocresol purple solution |

All adulterants (starch, gelatin, cane sugar, sucrose, calcium carbonate, sodium carbonate, sodium bicarbonate, urea, detergent powder) for preparation of positive control samples

## Procedures

Prepare a positive control sample for each test by adding respective adulterant in milk.

Carry out each test with the positive control and the test sample.

Compare the results of the test sample and the positive control.

### 6.1 Starch

Take 3 ml of milk sample in a test tube.

Boil it over a flame and then allow to cool to room temperature.

Add a drop of 1% iodine solution.

Appearance of a blue colour indicates the presence of starch.

### 6.2 Gelatin

Take 10 ml of milk in a large test tube

Add 10 ml of mercuric nitrate solution, shake and allow to stand for 5 minutes.

Filter in a test tube.

Opalescent filtrate indicates presence of gelatin.

Add equal amount of saturated aqueous picric acid solution.

Yellow precipitate indicates the presence of gelatin.

### 6.3 Cane sugar

Take about 15 ml of milk in a test tube.

Add 1 ml of concentrated HCl and 0.1g of resorcinol.

Mix and place the tube in a boiling water bath for 5 minutes.

Appearance of red colour indicates the presence of cane sugar.

### 6.4 Sucrose

Take 10 ml milk in a test tube.

Add resorcinol.

Development of red colour indicates the presence of sucrose.

### 6.5 Calcium carbonate

Take 10 ml of milk in a test tube

Add 1 ml of conc. HCl.

Effervescence indicates the presence of calcium carbonate.

### 6.6 Sodium bicarbonate or sodium carbonate (Rosalic acid test)

Take 5 ml of milk in a test tube.

Add 5 ml of alcohol followed by a few drops of 1% alcoholic solution of rosalic acid and mix.

Appearance of rose red colour suggests the presence of sodium bicarbonate or carbonate.

### 6.7 Urea

Take 5 ml of milk in a small conical flask.

Add 5 ml of 24% TCA solution.

Filter the mixture and collect the filtrate.

Take 1 ml of the filtrate in a test tube.

Add 1 ml of 2% NaOH solution followed by 0.5 ml of 2% sodium hypochlorite solution.

Mix and then add 0.5 ml of 5% phenol solution.

Appearance of a blue or bluish green colour indicates the presence of urea.

## 6.8 Detergent

Take 5 ml of milk in a test tube.

Add 0.1 ml of 0.5% bromocresol purple solution.

Development of violet colour indicates the presence of detergent while in the unadulterated milk there is development of faint violet colour.

## Interpretation

The presence of any extraneous matter that is not permissible in milk is considered as adulteration and the quality of milk may be declared unsatisfactory.

## Precautions

The glassware used in the tests should be clean and dry.

The chemicals should be handled carefully.

## Limitations

The tests are qualitative and not quantitative.

There may be other adulterants besides those listed above. More tests may be required to rule out the possibility of other adulterants.

**Record sheet** - Detection of adulterants in milk

| Sample No. | Adulterant | Observations | Test result | Interpretation |
|---|---|---|---|---|
| | Starch | | | |
| | Gelatin | | | |
| | Cane sugar | | | |
| | Sucrose | | | |
| | Calcium carbonate | | | |
| | Sodium bicarbonate or carbonates | | | |
| | Urea | | | |
| | Detergent | | | |
| | Starch | | | |
| | Gelatin | | | |
| | Cane sugar | | | |
| | Sucrose | | | |
| | Calcium carbonate | | | |
| | Sodium bicarbonate or carbonates | | | |
| | Urea | | | |
| | Detergent | | | |
| | Starch | | | |
| | Gelatin | | | |
| | Cane sugar | | | |
| | Sucrose | | | |
| | Calcium carbonate | | | |
| | Sodium bicarbonate or carbonates | | | |
| | Urea | | | |
| | Detergent | | | |

| | | | | |
|---|---|---|---|---|
| | Starch | | | |
| | Gelatin | | | |
| | Cane sugar | | | |
| | Sucrose | | | |
| | Calcium carbonate | | | |
| | Sodium bicarbonate or carbonates | | | |
| | Urea | | | |
| | Detergent | | | |
| | Starch | | | |
| | Gelatin | | | |
| | Cane sugar | | | |
| | Sucrose | | | |
| | Calcium carbonate | | | |
| | Sodium bicarbonate or carbonates | | | |
| | Urea | | | |
| | Detergent | | | |

Module 7

# Detection of preservatives in milk

A variety of chemical preservatives such as boric acid, borax, formaldehyde, hydrogen peroxide, salicylic acid etc. may be added by the milk producers to mask the unhygienic and insanitary conditions prevailing during milk production. Addition of preservative increases the keeping quality of milk by reducing the microbial population in it. These chemicals may be hazardous to consumers. Tests are necessary to confirm the absence of such illegal preservatives in milk before it is accepted for processing. All tests are based on specific chemical reactions between the preservatives present in the milk and thc diagnostic reagents.

## Apparatus

| | |
|---|---|
| Test tubes | Pipettes |
| Conical flasks | Porcelain dish |
| Water bath | Steam bath |

## Reagents

| | |
|---|---|
| Dried turmeric paper | Concentrated HCl |
| Concentrated $H_2SO_4$ | Ethyl ether |
| 0.5% ferric chloride solution, neutral | 2% paraphenylenediamine solution |
| Diluted HCl (1:3 by volume) | |

All preservatives (boric acid, formaldehyde, hydrogen peroxide, salicylic acid) for preparation of positive control samples

### Procedures

Prepare a positive control sample for each test by adding the respective preservative in a portion of milk.

Carry out each test with the positive control and the test samples.

Compare the results of the test sample with that of positive control.

## 7.1 Boric acid or borax (Turmeric paper test)

Take 100 ml of milk sample and acidify it by adding 7 ml of concentrated HCl.

Dip a strip of turmeric paper and allow it to dry.

The presence of boric acid or borax is indicated by the change in colour of the strip to red.

## 7.2 Formaldehyde (Hehner test)

Take 10 ml of milk in a wide test tube.

Add about 5 ml of concentrated sulphuric acid slowly along the wall of the tube so that it forms a layer at the bottom of the milk without mixing the two.

Appearance of violet or blue colour at the junction of the two liquids indicates the presence of formaldehyde.

## 7.3 Hydrogen peroxide

Take 5 ml of raw milk sample in a test tube.

Add 5 drops of 2% paraphenylenediamine solution.

Development of blue colour indicates the presence of hydrogen peroxide.

## 7.4 Salicylic acid (Ferric chloride test)

Take 100 ml of milk and add 5 ml of dilute HCl.

Shake the mixture until milk is curdled and filter.

Extract with 50-100 ml of ether.

Wash the ether layer twice with 5 ml water.

Pour it into a porcelain dish and keep on a steam bath to evaporate a major portion of ether.

Allow the remaining ether to evaporate off at room temperature.

Add one drop of 0.5% neutral ferric chloride solution.

The presence of salicylic acid is indicated by the development of a violet colour.

### Precautions

Glassware should be clean and dry.

Chemical solutions should be handled carefully.

### Limitations

Hydrogen peroxide may not be detected in milk that has been heat-treated or stored for long.

The tests are qualitative and not quantitative.

The milk may contain some other preservatives besides those listed above.

**Record sheet** - Detection of preservatives in milk

| Sample No. | Preservative | Observation | Test results | Interpretation |
|---|---|---|---|---|
| | Boric acid | | | |
| | Formaldehyde | | | |
| | Hydrogen peroxide | | | |
| | Salicylic acid | | | |
| | Boric acid | | | |
| | Formaldehyde | | | |
| | Hydrogen peroxide | | | |
| | Salicylic acid | | | |
| | Boric acid | | | |
| | Formaldehyde | | | |
| | Hydrogen peroxide | | | |
| | Salicylic acid | | | |
| | Boric acid | | | |
| | Formaldehyde | | | |
| | Hydrogen peroxide | | | |
| | Salicylic acid | | | |
| | Boric acid | | | |
| | Formaldehyde | | | |
| | Hydrogen peroxide | | | |
| | Salicylic acid | | | |

Module 8

# Isolation and identification of organisms of public health significance from milk and milk products

The examination of milk and dairy products for SPC, coliform bacteria, psychrotrophs and thermophiles etc. is quite useful in assessing the bacterial load and hygienic quality of the products. However, these methods cannot provide confirmatory evidence of presence of foodborne pathogens. With respect to food safety, the presence of pathogens in food may be very risky. Therefore, it becomes sometimes necessary to examine the dairy products for pathogens to rule out the presence of pathogenic organisms and to ensure consumer safety from foodborne illness.

## 8.1. Enumeration of *Staphylococcus aureus* (Time required: 2 days)

*Staphylococcus aureus* is an important pathogen commonly encountered in dairy products and in the outbreaks of foodborne illnesses due to consumption of contaminated dairy products. The enumeration of *S. aureus* helps in assessing the food associated health risk due to the organism. *S. aureus* in food sample is cultured and enumerated on Baird-Parker agar medium which is a selective medium. The organisms grow and form typical colonies on the culture medium. The colonies are grey to black in colour with off white margin surrounded by an opaque zone and usually surrounded by an outer clear zone. The colonies are circular, convex, smooth and 2-3 mm in diameter.

### 8.1.1 Apparatus

| | |
|---|---|
| Petri dishes | Burner |
| Pipettes | Marker pen |
| Test tubes with test tube stand | Incubator at 37➡C |
| Spreader (L-shaped glass rod) | Water bath at 45-50➡C |
| Beaker | |

### 8.1.2 Culture media/reagents

**(a) Baird-Parker agar base with egg yolk tellurite enrichment**

| | | |
|---|---|---|
| Pancreatic digest of casein | : | 10 g |
| Beef extract | : | 5 g |
| Yeast extract | : | 1 g |
| Glycine | : | 12 g |
| Sodium pyruvate | : | 10 g |
| Lithium chloride | : | 5 g |
| Agar agar | : | 20 g |

Suspend the above ingredients in 950 ml of distilled water. Heat to dissolve and boil for one minute. Autoclave and after cooling to 45-50°C, add 50 ml of egg yolk tellurite emulsion consisting of 30% egg yolk suspension with 0.15% potassium tellurite. Mix thoroughly but gently.

**(b) Sterile 0.85% saline solution**

Dissolve 8.5 grams of sodium chloride in 1 liter of distilled water and autoclave to sterilize. Dispense 9 ml solution into test tubes.

**(c) Spirit or ethanol in beaker**

### 8.1.3 Procedure

Prepare serial decimal dilutions of the sample as described in the standard plate count (SPC) test or in the examination of dairy products for hygienic quality.

Inoculate Baird-Parker agar medium plates in duplicate with 0.1 ml of the sample dilutions by surface plating.

For surface spreading, take a spreader, dip it in spirit and flame it to sterilize. Cool it by holding for few seconds.

Touch the bent portion of the spreader on culture medium in the plate to cool it down completely.

Spread the inoculum on each plate with sterile spreader.

Incubate the plates at 37°C for 48 hours.

### 8.1.4 Observations and recording of results

Select the set of plates of the same dilution showing colony forming units between 15 and 150.

Count the number of colonies with typical characters of *S. aureus*.

Calculate the number per ml by taking into account the dilution factor.

### 8.1.5 Interpretation

The product should meet the safety requirements of Food Safety and Standards Regulations, 2011 mentioned in Table 8.1.

The presence of *S. aureus* may be due to insufficient heat processing of the product or its contamination during subsequent handling.

High *S. aureus* count indicates unsatisfactory quality of the product.

Very high count indicates the possibility of growth of the microorganisms having taken place in the products during storage, resulting in the chances of enterotoxin production in the product.

### 8.1.6 Precautions

Colony count should be preferred in uncrowded plates.

The colonies of injured or stressed bacterial cells may slightly differ from those of the typical colonies.

The spreader after flaming should be adequately cooled down before touching with the inoculated sample.

### 8.1.7 Limitations

The colonies reveal presumptive *S. aureus* organism which may require further confirmation.

The test does not reveal the status of food in terms of staphylococcal enterotoxin.

**Table 8.1 Microbiological requirements concerning pathogenic bacteria in processed milk and milk products according to the Food Safety and Standards (Food Products Standards and Food Additives) Regulations, 2011 (India)**

| Product (n=5) | Sampling plan | *Escherichia coli* | *Salmonella* | *Staph. aureus* (coagulase +ve) | *Listeria monocytogenes* |
|---|---|---|---|---|---|
| Pasteurised milk, cream, flavoured milk | M | Absent/g | Absent/ 25g | <10/g | Absent/g |
| Sweetened condensed milk | m | - | - | 10/g (c=2) | - |
| | M | Absent/g | Absent/25g | 100/g | Absent/g |
| Pasteurised butter | m | - | - | 10/g (c=2) | - |
| | M | Absent/g | Absent/25g | 50/g | Absent/g |
| Dried products: milk powder, cream, whey, edible casein, ice cream mix | M | Absent/g | Absent/25g | <10/g | Absent/g |

| Product (n=5) | Sampling plan | *Escherichia coli* | *Salmonella* | *Staph. aureus* (coagulase +ve) | *Listeria monocytogenes* |
|---|---|---|---|---|---|
| Ice cream, frozen dessert, milk lolly, ice candy | M | Absent/g | Absent/25g | <10/g | Absent/g |
| Processed cheese, cheese spread | M | Absent/g | Absent/25g | <10/g | Absent/g |
| All other cheeses | m | - | - | 100/g (c=2) | - |
| | M | <10/g | Absent/g | 1000/g | Hard cheese- Absent/g, Other cheeses- Absent/25g |
| Yoghurt, dahi, chakka, shrikhand | m | - | - | 50/g (c=2) | - |
| | M | Absent/g | Absent/25g | 100/g | Absent/g |
| Paneer, chhana | m | - | - | 50/g (c=2) | - |
| | M | <10/g | Absent/g | 100/g | Absent/g |
| Khoya | m | - | - | 50/g (c=2) | - |
| | M | <10/g | Absent/25g | 100/g | Absent/g |

n = The number of sample units which must be examined from the batch/lot of food.

m = Represents an acceptable level and values above it are marginally acceptable in terms of the sampling plan.

M = A microbiological criterion which separates marginally acceptable quality from unsatisfactory/potentially hazardous quality. Values above M are unacceptable and detection of one or more samples exceeding this level would be cause for rejection of the lot.

c = The maximum allowable number of defective sample units which may exceed the microbiological limit

n = The number of sample units which must be examined from the batch/lot of food to satisfy the requirements of a particular sampling plan specified by m.

## Illustration

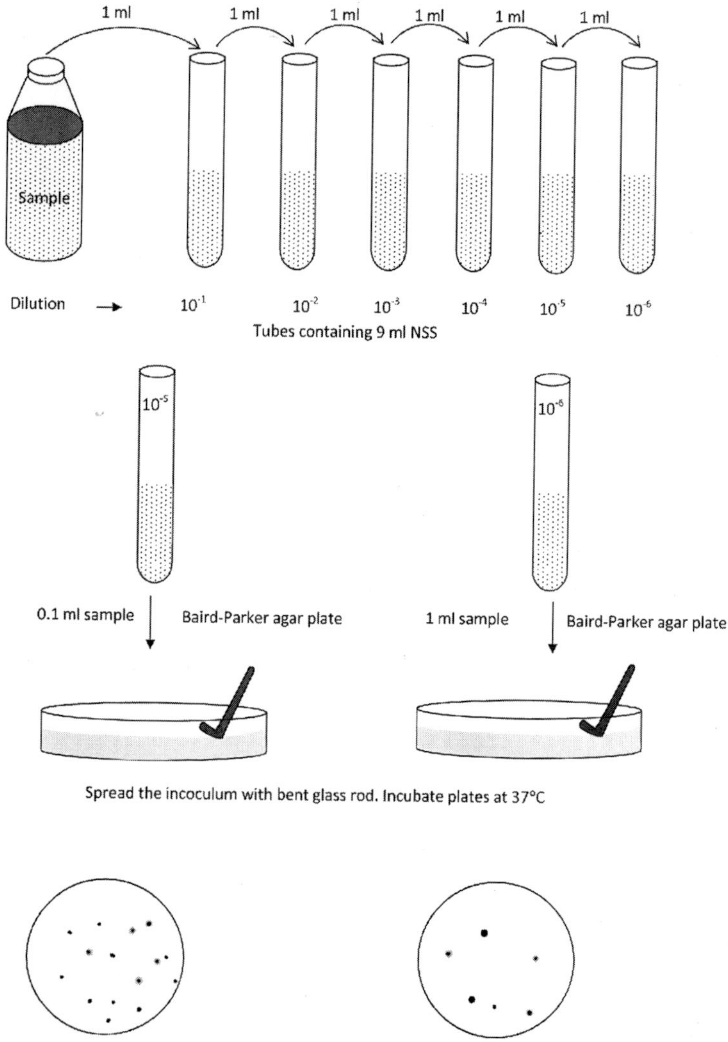


Staphylococcal colonies on Baird-Parker Agar

**Record sheet** - Enumeration of *S. aureus*

| Sample No. | Dilution | Colony count | | | Dilution factor | cfu/ml | Interpretation |
|---|---|---|---|---|---|---|---|
| | | Plate I | Plate II | Average | | | |
| | $10^{-1}$ | | | | $10^{1}$ | | |
| | $10^{-2}$ | | | | $10^{2}$ | | |
| | $10^{-3}$ | | | | $10^{3}$ | | |
| | $10^{-4}$ | | | | $10^{4}$ | | |
| | $10^{-5}$ | | | | $10^{5}$ | | |
| | $10^{-6}$ | | | | $10^{6}$ | | |
| | $10^{-1}$ | | | | $10^{1}$ | | |
| | $10^{-2}$ | | | | $10^{2}$ | | |
| | $10^{-3}$ | | | | $10^{3}$ | | |
| | $10^{-4}$ | | | | $10^{4}$ | | |
| | $10^{-5}$ | | | | $10^{5}$ | | |
| | $10^{-6}$ | | | | $10^{6}$ | | |
| | $10^{-1}$ | | | | $10^{1}$ | | |
| | $10^{-2}$ | | | | $10^{2}$ | | |
| | $10^{-3}$ | | | | $10^{3}$ | | |
| | $10^{-4}$ | | | | $10^{4}$ | | |
| | $10^{-5}$ | | | | $10^{5}$ | | |
| | $10^{-6}$ | | | | $10^{6}$ | | |
| | $10^{-1}$ | | | | $10^{1}$ | | |
| | $10^{-2}$ | | | | $10^{2}$ | | |
| | $10^{-3}$ | | | | $10^{3}$ | | |
| | $10^{-4}$ | | | | $10^{4}$ | | |
| | $10^{-5}$ | | | | $10^{5}$ | | |
| | $10^{-6}$ | | | | $10^{6}$ | | |

## 8.2. Detection of *Salmonella* (Time required: 4-5 days)

Salmonellosis is a major public health problem affecting man and animals throughout the world. A large number of serotypes of *Salmonella* are widely distributed in nature. Unhygienically processed dairy products can act as potential source of *Salmonella*. Food laws of most of the countries prohibit its presence in any food. Isolation of *Salmonella* is quite challenging as the organisms may be present in small numbers. Therefore, isolation methodology involves several steps such as pre-enrichment, enrichment and selective plating to increase the chance of detection of the organism or to completely rule out the possibility of its presence in the food.

### 8.2.1 Apparatus

| | |
|---|---|
| Conical flasks (250 ml) | Petri dishes |
| Pipettes | Inoculation loop |
| Test tubes | Water bath |
| Incubator | Marking pen |
| Bunsen burner | |

### 8.2.2 Culture media/reagents

#### (a) Buffered peptone water

| | | |
|---|---|---|
| Peptone | : | 10 g |
| Sodium chloride | : | 5 g |
| Disodium phosphate | : | 3.5 g |
| Monopotassium phosphate | : | 1.5 g |

Suspend all the ingredients in 1 L distilled water and mix thoroughly. Warm gently until solution is complete. Dispense 225 ml quantities in conical flasks and then autoclave at 121°C for 15 minutes.

## (b) Tetrathionate broth

| | | |
|---|---|---|
| Proteose peptone | : | 2.5 g |
| Pancreatic digest of casein | : | 2.5 g |
| Bile salts | : | 1 g |
| Sodium thiosulfate | : | 30 g |
| Calcium carbonate | : | 10 g |

Suspend the above ingredients in 1 L distilled water. Heat to boiling and then cool to below 60°C. Distribute the medium in 100 ml quantities. To 100 ml portion of the medium add 2 ml of iodine solution (prepared by dissolving 6 g of iodine crystals and 5 g of potassium iodide in 20 ml of water). Do not reheat the medium after adding iodine. Do not autoclave. This medium is for immediate use only.

## (c) Brilliant green agar (BGA)

| | | |
|---|---|---|
| Proteose peptone No. 3 | : | 10 g |
| Yeast extract | : | 3 g |
| Lactose | : | 10 g |
| Saccharose | : | 10 g |
| Sodium chloride | : | 5 g |
| Brilliant green | : | 12.5 mg |
| Phenol red | : | 80 mg |
| Agar agar | : | 20 g |

Suspend all the ingredients in 1 L of distilled water and mix thoroughly. Heat with frequent agitation and boil for 1 minute to completely dissolve the powder. Autoclave at 121°C for 15 minutes. Dispense in sterile petri plates.

(d) **Triple sugar iron agar slants**

(e) **Media and reagents for biochemical tests**

(f) ***Salmonella* polyvalent somatic (O) and flagellar (H) antisera**

### 8.2.3 Procedure

Inoculate 25 ml or 25 g product sample aseptically into 225 ml of lactose broth in a flask for preenrichment. Mix and incubate for 24 h at 35➡C

Transfer 1 ml preenriched sample to 10 ml of tetrathionate broth and incubate at 35➡C for 24 h for selective enrichment. Note that the control of temperature is critical at this step.

Streak the enriched culture on selective medium BGA plate with loop and incubate for 24 h at 37➡C

Pick up suspected colony(ies) from the selective medium and inoculate into triple sugar iron agar slant for further identification. Incubate at 37➡C for 24h.

Isolates showing alkaline slant (pink) and acidic butt (yellow) with or without $H_2S$ production (blackening) are processed further.

Further confirmation should be done by studying biochemical characteristics of the suspected isolates.

Confirmation of suspected isolates should be done with polyvalent *Salmonella* antiserum by slide agglutination test.

### 8.2.4 Observations and recording of results

The isolates subjected to each of the biochemical test should be observed and results should be recorded positive or negative as the case may be.

Isolates showing typical biochemical reactions for *Salmonella* genus as shown in record sheet Table are considered as *Salmonella*. Hence the sample from which such isolate is obtained is considered as positive for *Salmonella*.

### 8.2.5 Interpretation

*Salmonella* should be absent in 25 g sample of dairy products (Table 8.1) in all food items. The presence of *Salmonella* indicates the food products should be rejected.

### 8.2.6 Precautions

Results should not be declared on the basis of colony morphology alone without identifying the isolates biochemically and serologically.

### 8.2.7 Limitation

The test requires very long period.

**Record sheet** - Detection of *Salmonella*

| Sample details | Isolate No. | Colony characteristics | Gram's reaction (-) | Reaction on TSI agar | $H_2S$ in TSI agar | Motility (+) | Lysine decarboxylase (+) | Nitrate reduction (-) | Indole (-) | Methyl red (+) | VP (-) | Urease (-) | Malonate (-) | Polyvalent O antisera (+) | Polyvalent H antisera (+) | Interpretation |
|---|---|---|---|---|---|---|---|---|---|---|---|---|---|---|---|---|
| | | | | | | | | | | | | | | | | |
| | | | | | | | | | | | | | | | | |
| | | | | | | | | | | | | | | | | |
| | | | | | | | | | | | | | | | | |
| | | | | | | | | | | | | | | | | |
| | | | | | | | | | | | | | | | | |
| | | | | | | | | | | | | | | | | |
| | | | | | | | | | | | | | | | | |
| | | | | | | | | | | | | | | | | |
| | | | | | | | | | | | | | | | | |
| | | | | | | | | | | | | | | | | |
| | | | | | | | | | | | | | | | | |
| | | | | | | | | | | | | | | | | |
| | | | | | | | | | | | | | | | | |
| | | | | | | | | | | | | | | | | |
| | | | | | | | | | | | | | | | | |
| | | | | | | | | | | | | | | | | |
| | | | | | | | | | | | | | | | | |
| | | | | | | | | | | | | | | | | |
| | | | | | | | | | | | | | | | | |

| | | | | | | | | | | | | | | | | |
|---|---|---|---|---|---|---|---|---|---|---|---|---|---|---|---|---|
| | | | | | | | | | | | | | | | | |
| | | | | | | | | | | | | | | | | |
| | | | | | | | | | | | | | | | | |
| | | | | | | | | | | | | | | | | |

***Note***: Reactions of typical *Salmonella* are shown in parenthesis, - negative, + positive

## 8.3. Enumeration of *Bacillus cereus* (Time required: 2 days)

*Bacillus cereus* is a spore forming organism commonly found in the environment. Due to toxigenic nature of the bacteria, it is an important food poisoning agent.

### 8.3.1 Apparatus

| | |
|---|---|
| Petri dishes with culture medium | Sterile pipettes |
| Test tubes | Test tube rack |
| Spreader (L-shaped glass rod) | Beaker |
| Incubator at 37°C | Burner |
| Marking pen | |

### 8.3.2 Culture media/reagents

### (a) Mannitol egg yolk polymyxin agar (MEYP)

| | | |
|---|---|---|
| Beef extract | : | 1 g |
| Peptone | : | 10 g |
| D-Mannitol | : | 10 g |
| Sodium chloride | : | 10 g |
| Phenol red | : | 25 mg |
| Agar | : | 20 g |

Suspend 46 g of dehydrated powder of above mentioned composition in 900 ml distilled water. Mix thoroughly and heat with frequent agitation and boil for 1 minute to completely dissolve the powder. Dispense 225 ml into 500 ml flasks and then autoclave at 121°C for 15 minutes. Cool to 45-50°C. Aseptically add 12.5 ml of 50% egg yolk suspension and quantity of polymyxin equivalent to 25,000 IU. Mix thoroughly and then prepare plates.

**(b) Sterile 0.85% saline solution**

### 8.3.3 Procedure

Weigh 10 g sample and homogenize with 90 ml diluent (saline solution) and make further 10-fold serial dilutions.

Inoculate 0.1 ml from each dilution by spread technique on the culture medium plates in duplicate and incubate the plates at 37→C.

*B. cereus* forms pink-red colonies with an opaque zone of turbidity.

### 8.3.4 Observations and recording of results

Count the colony forming units in an appropriate dilution.

Calculate the bacterial count per ml by taking into account the dilution factor.

### 8.3.5 Interpretation

Determine the quality of the product based on the guidelines/ standards for that particular product.

### 8.3.6 Precautions

While making the medium, care should be taken to add egg yolk and polymyxin B sulphate to the base medium cooled down to 45-50→C.

## 8.3.7 Limitation

The test may not be able to detect the presence of bacteria when present in very small number in food.

**Record sheet -** Enumeration of *B. cereus*

| Sample No. | Dilution | Colony count | | | Dilution factor | cfu/g | Interpretation |
|---|---|---|---|---|---|---|---|
| | | Plate I | Plate II | Average | | | |
| | $10^{-1}$ | | | | $10^{1}$ | | |
| | $10^{-2}$ | | | | $10^{2}$ | | |
| | $10^{-3}$ | | | | $10^{3}$ | | |
| | $10^{-4}$ | | | | $10^{4}$ | | |
| | $10^{-5}$ | | | | $10^{5}$ | | |
| | $10^{-6}$ | | | | $10^{6}$ | | |
| | $10^{-1}$ | | | | $10^{1}$ | | |
| | $10^{-2}$ | | | | $10^{2}$ | | |
| | $10^{-3}$ | | | | $10^{3}$ | | |
| | $10^{-4}$ | | | | $10^{4}$ | | |
| | $10^{-5}$ | | | | $10^{5}$ | | |
| | $10^{-6}$ | | | | $10^{6}$ | | |
| | $10^{-1}$ | | | | $10^{1}$ | | |
| | $10^{-2}$ | | | | $10^{2}$ | | |
| | $10^{-3}$ | | | | $10^{3}$ | | |
| | $10^{-4}$ | | | | $10^{4}$ | | |
| | $10^{-5}$ | | | | $10^{5}$ | | |
| | $10^{-6}$ | | | | $10^{6}$ | | |
| | $10^{-1}$ | | | | $10^{1}$ | | |
| | $10^{-2}$ | | | | $10^{2}$ | | |
| | $10^{-3}$ | | | | $10^{3}$ | | |
| | $10^{-4}$ | | | | $10^{4}$ | | |
| | $10^{-5}$ | | | | $10^{5}$ | | |
| | $10^{-6}$ | | | | $10^{6}$ | | |

Module 9

# Detection of antimicrobial residues and toxic chemicals in foods

The use of a number of drugs for therapeutic purpose or for promoting growth of the animals is quite common in the modern animal husbandry practices. These include antimicrobials, hormones, tranquilizers etc. The animals are also exposed to many environmental contaminants such as pesticides, herbicides, heavy metals etc. The residues of these chemicals may appear in the foods originating from such animals, many of which may be harmful to the consumers.

Antimicrobial drugs constitute a major category of such chemicals of public health concern. Antimicrobial residues in foods give rise to the problem of development of antimicrobial resistant strains of bacteria and their spread through food chain. Certain agents may also cause allergic reactions among the sensitive people.

Antimicrobial residues can be detected by simple test based on inhibition of growth of bacteria by the antimicrobial residues. However, the detection of other toxic chemicals may require specialized equipments and techniques such as chromatography, immunoassays, spectrographic methods etc.

## 9.1 Test for antimicrobial residues in milk (Time required: 24 h)

Antimicrobial residues present in milk inhibit the growth of *Sarcina lutea* in culture medium. The formation of clear zones of inhibition by the milk samples inoculated with bacterial cultures after overnight incubation indicates the presence of antimicrobial residues.

### 9.1.1 Apparatus

| | | |
|---|---|---|
| Sterile petri dishes | Desiccators | Well-cutter |
| Refrigerator | Incubator at 30°C | Filter paper |

### 9.1.2 Culture medium/reagent

Meat extract peptone agar in petri dish

Meat extract peptone broth

0.85% saline solution

### 9.1.3 Bacterial culture

*Sarcina lutea*, 24 hour culture in meat extract peptone broth

### 9.1.4 Procedure

Take a freshly prepared plate of meat extract peptone agar and dry it in a desiccator for two hours to remove moisture.

Inoculate the agar plate with 0.1-0.2 ml of *Sarcina lutea* culture by spread plate method and dry the uncovered plate for 30 minutes in a desiccator.

Cut wells in the agar with well-cutter.

Seal the bottom of each well with melted agar medium.

Charge the wells with the milk samples.

Place the plates in the refrigerator at 4°C for 2 hours to allow diffusion of samples in the agar.

Put moistened filter paper in the lid to avoid excessive drying of culture medium.

Incubate the petri dish at 30°C for 16-18 hours.

### 9.1.5 Observations and recording of results

Observe the plate for clear zones of inhibition of growth of the test culture around the wells and record the results.

### 9.1.6 Interpretation

Zone of inhibition surrounding a well indicates the presence of antimicrobial residues in the sample.

### 9.1.6 Precautions

Test culture should be in log phase of growth and should not be old.

In case of dense growth, the bacterial culture should be diluted in sterile 0.85% saline solution.

### 9.1.7 Limitation

The zone of inhibition indicates the presence of antimicrobial residues but it does not tell about the identity of the substance.

**Record sheet -** Test for antimicrobial residues in milk

| Sample details | Diameter of clear zone of inhibition | Result | Interpretation |
|---|---|---|---|
| | | | |
| | | | |
| | | | |
| | | | |
| | | | |

Module 10

# Evaluation of dairy plant sanitation

The hygienic quality of a dairy product depends upon the sanitary conditions prevailing in the milk processing plant. It is very important to maintain the equipment and containers in the plant under very strictly controlled sanitary conditions to prevent contamination of products. The quality of water and air in the dairy plant also needs due care to prevent contamination of the products. Hence, it is important to regularly evaluate the sanitary conditions in the dairy plant by conducting microbiological examination of equipment, containers and the environment.

## 10.1 Evaluation of equipment sanitation

Good sanitation practices require the product contact surfaces of all multiuse containers, equipment and utensils used in the handling, storage or transportation of milk to be cleaned after each usage and to be sanitized prior to reuse. It is, therefore, necessary to assess the efficiency of sanitation process. Rinse solution method and the swab contact method are used to collect the samples for laboratory examination for microbiological quality.

### 10.1.1 Apparatus

| | |
|---|---|
| Sterile petri dishes | Sterile pipettes |
| Sterile hypodermic syringe | Test tube rack |
| Test tubes | Sterile swabs |
| Incubator at 37°C | Beaker |
| Marking pen | Burner |

### 10.1.2 Culture medium/reagents

Plate count agar (Same as in Section 4.2.2)

Normal saline solution (Same as in Section 4.2.2)

### 10.1.3 Procedure

For metal containers, introduce measured quantity (20-50 ml) of normal saline solution into the container. Shake the container vigorously vertically, horizontally and in circular direction so that the rinsing solution comes into contact with entire surface. Collect the rinsing solution in sterile vials.

In case of flexible plastic containers which are formed, filled and sealed in a single device, obtain the container just prior to the introduction of product. With the help of sterile hypodermic syringe, introduce the rinsing solution into sealed bag and apply a piece of cellophane tape to cover the punctured area. Shake the bag vigorously. Cut the bag at the corner and pour the content into sterile vials.

For big containers like milk cans and big equipments, collect the sample by swab method. For this moisten the swab with sterile normal saline solution and then rub the swab head slowly and thoroughly over 5 $cm^2$ area. Then return the swab head to a vial containing measured (5-10 ml) volume of sterile normal saline solution. Rinse the swab briefly in solution then press out the absorbed solution before the swab is removed.

Once all the above mentioned samples are brought to the laboratory, proceed for the microbiological examination in a similar way detailed elsewhere i.e. standard plate count (Section 4.2), psychrophiles and psychrotrophs count (Section 4.3), thermophiles count (Section 4.4) and coliform bacteria count (Section 4.5) etc.

### 10.1.4 Observations and recording of results

Observe the petri dishes for the presence of colonies on the respective culture media and count the colony forming units.

Multiply the number with dilution factor and express the results in appropriate units e.g. cfu/ml or cfu/cm$^2$.

### 10.1.5 Interpretation

Interpret the results on the basis of the available recommendations and guidelines.

### 10.1.6 Precautions

Take all precautions for asepsis while collecting the samples.

### 10.1.7 Limitation

All the microorganisms may not be detached from the surfaces by rinsing or swabbing, hence the results do not give true microbial load.

**Record sheet** - Evaluation of equipment sanitation

| Sample No. | Sample details | Standard plate count | Psychrophiles and psychrotrophs | Thermophiles | Coliforms | Interpre-tation |
|---|---|---|---|---|---|---|
| | | | | | | |
| | | | | | | |
| | | | | | | |
| | | | | | | |
| | | | | | | |

## 10.2 Evaluation of microbiological quality of water (Time required: 24-48 h)

Water used in dairy plants and milk processing centers should be clean and uncontaminated. The quality of water is monitored by testing it for coliform organisms and standard plate count. Coliform bacteria are indicators of faecal contamination of water. Coliform count test is done by multiple tube method described below while the standard plate count test can be conducted as described for milk (Section 4.2).

Multiple tube method provides an estimation of coliform bacteria in water sample as most probable number (MPN)/100 ml. The test involves addition of varying quantities of water to the culture medium MacConkey's broth. The medium contains bromocresol purple to indicate acid production in the medium due to the growth of coliform bacteria. The culture medium tube also has a Durham's tube inserted in an inverted position to show the formation of gas. The presence of coliforms in water sample is demonstrated by production of acid and gas on fermentation of lactose at 37➡C for 24-48 h and their MPN is recorded with the help of McCrady's Probability Table.

### 10.2.1 Apparatus

| | |
|---|---|
| Test tubes | Conical flasks |
| Test tube stand | Incubator |
| Durham's tubes | Pipettes (1 ml, 5 ml, 10 ml) |
| Marker pen | McCardy's Probability Table |

### 10.2.2 Culture media/reagents

### (a) MacConkey's broth (Single strength)

| | | |
|---|---|---|
| Oxgall (bile salts) | : | 5 g |
| Pancreatic digest of gelatin | : | 20 g |
| Lactose | : | 10 g |
| Bromcresol purple | : | 0.01 g |

Dissolve in 1 L of distilled water and dispense in 5 ml amounts in test tubes with inverted Durham's tube and autoclave at 121→C for 15 minutes.

### (b) MacConkey's broth (Double strength)

Take double the quantity of each of the above ingredients and dissolve in 1000 ml of distilled water. Dispense 10 ml quantities in 25-30 ml capacity test tubes with inverted Durham's tube and autoclave at 121→C for 15 minutes.

### 10.2.3 Procedure

Take a set of 3 test tubes containing 10 ml double strength MacConkey's broth and two sets of 3 test tubes each containing 5 ml single strength MacConkey's broth medium.

Mark these as Set I, Set II and Set III and arrange them in a test tube stand.

Shake the water sample thoroughly. Add 10 ml water sample aseptically in each test tube of the Set I. Add 1 ml sample in each tube of the Set II and 0.1 ml in the Set III tubes.

Mix and incubate the tubes at 37→C for 24 h.

### 10.2.4 Observations and recording of results

Observc the inoculated test tubes for the change in colour of the medium from purple to yellow indicating acid production.

Observe each tube for the production of gas. Accumulation of gas in Durham's tube to fill its concavity indicates gas production.

A tube showing both the above reactions i.e. acid and gas production after 24-48 h incubation is taken as positive for presumptive coliforms.

Record the number of positive tubes (out of 3) in each set.

Determine the MPN of coliform bacteria per 100 ml of water sample from the McCrady's Probability Table as given in Table 10.1

### 10.2.5 Interpretation

Compare the results with the available guidelines for assessing suitability or non-suitability of the water sample for particular purpose. Drinking water should ideally have zero coliforms per 100 ml.

### 10.2.6 Precautions

Avoid trapping of air inside Durham's tube while inserting it in MacConkey's broth tubes.

The tubes showing negative reaction on incubation at 37➡C for 24 h should be further incubated for another 24 h and rechecked.

A tube showing acid production alone without gas production should not be taken as positive for coliforms.

Gas production should be considered positive only when at least the concavity of Durham's tube is filled with gas bubble.

### 10.2.7 Limitation

The test is based on probability, hence, gives most probable numbers of coliforms in the sample.

## Illustration

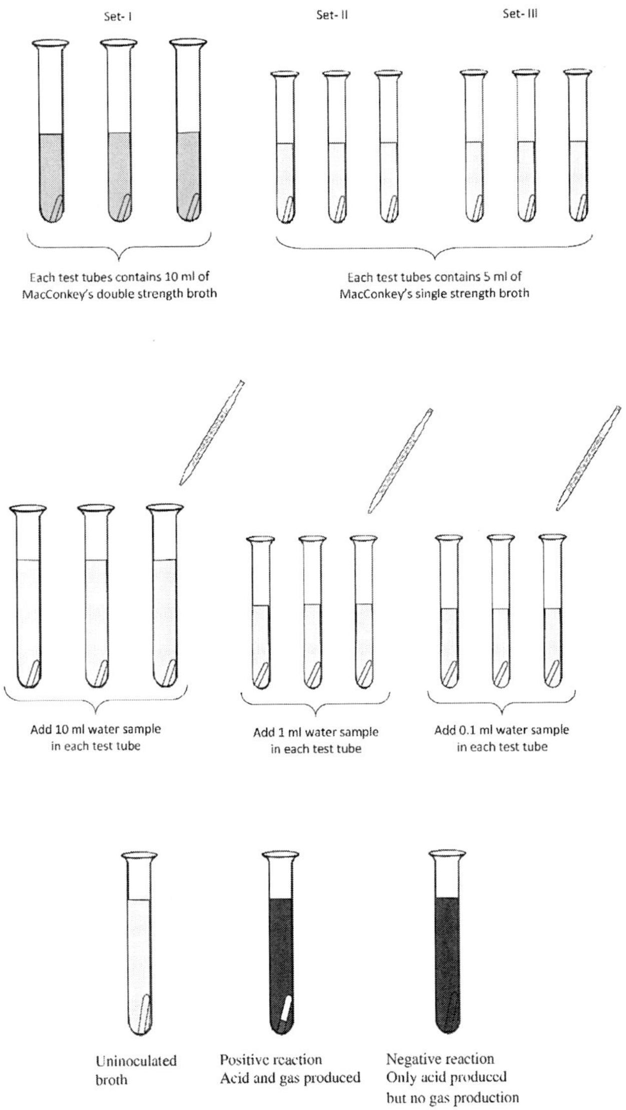

**Table 10.1 McCrady's probability table**
**Most probable number of coliforms in water with 3 tubes method**

| Tubes positive | | | MPN per 100 ml | Tubes positive | | | MPN per 100 ml |
|---|---|---|---|---|---|---|---|
| 10 ml | 1 ml | 0.1 ml | | 10 ml | 1 ml | 0.1 ml | |
| 0 | 0 | 0 | <3 | 2 | 0 | 0 | 9 |
| 0 | 0 | 1 | 3 | 2 | 0 | 1 | 14 |
| 0 | 0 | 2 | 6 | 2 | 0 | 2 | 20 |
| 0 | 0 | 3 | 9 | 2 | 0 | 3 | 26 |
| 0 | 1 | 0 | 3 | 2 | 1 | 0 | 15 |
| 0 | 1 | 1 | 6 | 2 | 1 | 1 | 20 |
| 0 | 1 | 2 | 9 | 2 | 1 | 2 | 27 |
| 0 | 1 | 3 | 12 | 2 | 1 | 3 | 34 |
| 0 | 2 | 0 | 6 | 2 | 2 | 0 | 21 |
| 0 | 2 | 1 | 9 | 2 | 2 | 1 | 28 |
| 0 | 2 | 2 | 12 | 2 | 2 | 2 | 35 |
| 0 | 2 | 3 | 16 | 2 | 2 | 3 | 42 |
| 0 | 3 | 0 | 9 | 2 | 3 | 0 | 29 |
| 0 | 3 | 1 | 13 | 2 | 3 | 1 | 36 |
| 0 | 3 | 2 | 16 | 2 | 3 | 2 | 44 |
| 0 | 3 | 3 | 19 | 2 | 3 | 3 | 53 |
| 1 | 0 | 0 | 4 | 3 | 0 | 0 | 23 |
| 1 | 0 | 1 | 7 | 3 | 0 | 1 | 39 |
| 1 | 0 | 2 | 11 | 3 | 0 | 2 | 64 |
| 1 | 0 | 3 | 15 | 3 | 0 | 3 | 95 |
| 1 | 1 | 0 | 7 | 3 | 1 | 0 | 43 |
| 1 | 1 | 1 | 11 | 3 | 1 | 1 | 75 |
| 1 | 1 | 2 | 15 | 3 | 1 | 2 | 120 |
| 1 | 1 | 3 | 19 | 3 | 1 | 3 | 160 |

| Tubes positive | | | MPN per 100 ml | Tubes positive | | | MPN per 100 ml |
|---|---|---|---|---|---|---|---|
| 10 ml | 1 ml | 0.1 ml | | 10 ml | 1 ml | 0.1 ml | |
| 1 | 2 | 0 | 11 | 3 | 2 | 0 | 93 |
| 1 | 2 | 1 | 15 | 3 | 2 | 1 | 150 |
| 1 | 2 | 2 | 20 | 3 | 2 | 2 | 210 |
| 1 | 2 | 3 | 24 | 3 | 2 | 3 | 290 |
| 1 | 3 | 0 | 16 | 3 | 3 | 0 | 240 |
| 1 | 3 | 1 | 20 | 3 | 3 | 1 | 460 |
| 1 | 3 | 2 | 24 | 3 | 3 | 2 | 1100 |
| 1 | 3 | 3 | 29 | 3 | 3 | 3 | >1100 |

**Record sheet -** Evaluation of water quality

| Sample details | Number of positive tubes (acid and gas) | | | Coliform (MPN/100 ml) | SPC/ml | Interpretation |
|---|---|---|---|---|---|---|
| | Set I 10 ml | Set II 1 ml | Set III 0.1 ml | | | |
| | | | | | | |
| | | | | | | |
| | | | | | | |
| | | | | | | |
| | | | | | | |

## 10.3 Bacteriological examination of air (Time required: 24 h)

There is a relationship between the microbiological quality of air and the number and types of microorganisms present in the dairy products exposed to the surrounding air.

The microorganisms present in the air are usually associated with dust particles, droplets or droplet nuclei in the environment. Depending upon their size and agitation of air, these either settle down or remain suspended. The bacterial load in the air can be determined with the help of specially designed air samplers. Air samplers grab a sample of known volume of air from an area which is directed to a culture medium plate. The microbes present in the air are impinged with force on the culture medium plate. Petri dish is then removed from the sampler and incubated at a suitable temperature. The colony forming units are counted and expressed as colony forming units per cubic meter (cfu/$m^3$) of air sample.

### 10.3.1 Apparatus

Air sampler

Petri plates with nutrient agar

Incubator

### 10.3.2 Reagents/media

Nutrient agar

| | | |
|---|---|---|
| Beef extract | : | 3 g |
| Peptone | : | 5 g |
| Agar | : | 15 g |

Suspend all the above ingredients in 1000 ml of distilled water. Mix thoroughly and heat with frequent agitation and boil for 1 minute to completely dissolve. Autoclave at 121→C for 15 minutes. Prepare petri plates of nutrient agar.

### 10.3.3 Procedure

Place the air sampler in a proper position at the place where air sample is required to be collected.

Place a petri plate of nutrient agar medium without lid at the designated place in the apparatus.

Operate the instrument for a predetermined time based on the volume of the air sample to be examined.

Record the volume of air sample used for examination.

Immediately put the cover of the petri plate, remove and place it in the incubator at 37°C for 24 h.

### 10.3.4 Observations and recording of results

After completion of the incubation period, observe the colonies developed on the culture medium and count all the visible colonies.

Express the result as cfu/$m^3$ by dividing the number of colony forming units with the volume of air (in cubic meters) used for analysis.

### 10.3.5 Interpretation

The interpretation of the results can be done on the basis of the prescribed standards/ guidelines for a particular type of establishment.

### 10.3.6 Precautions

Conduct the test in still air in an enclosure/ room without agitating the air.

### 10.3.7 Limitation

The test reveals total microbial load in the air but cannot tell the details of the microorganisms. However, different culture media may be used for different organisms.

**Illustration - Working of air sampler**

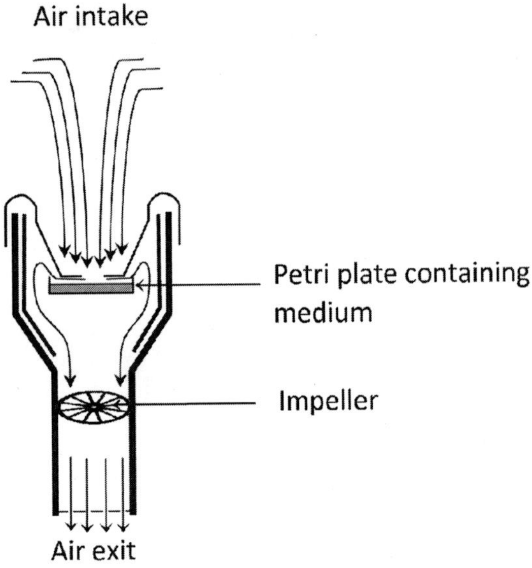


**Record sheet** - Bacteriological examination of air

| Sample details | Volume of air | cfu | cfu/m$^3$ | Interpretation |
|---|---|---|---|---|
| | | | | |
| | | | | |
| | | | | |
| | | | | |
| | | | | |

Module 11

# Ante-mortem inspection of food animals in abattoir

To ensure consumer safety, it is utmost important that only healthy and physiologically normal animals are slaughtered for meat production. Sick or doubtful animals should be segregated and should not be passed for slaughter until it is ascertained that the meat from such animals will be wholesome and will not pose risk to human health.

This objective can be achieved only by conducting strict ante-mortem examination of live animals brought for slaughter. Ante-mortem examination is important not only for the sake of meat consumers but also for animal welfare. Ante-mortem examination also helps in protecting the abattoir workers from transmission of zoonotic diseases from sick animals.

## 11.1 Purposes of ante-mortem inspection

- Protection of public health from transmissible infectious diseases
- Protection of public health from toxic residues in meat
- Protection from spread of infectious diseases particularly notifiable diseases among the livestock in the area
- Animal disease data feed back to farms or animal husbandry department of the region from which animals have originated
- Protection of animal handlers against zoonoses through feed back to the place of origin of the animals
- Protection of abattoir workers and meat handlers against zoonotic diseases

- Ensuring superior quality meat supply for consumer protection against cheating
- Prevention of contamination of slaughterhouse premises, equipment and meat by allowing clean animals for slaughter
- Collection of material for disease investigation and research

## 11.2 Objectives of ante-mortem inspection

- To screen animals for health status before slaughter
- To ensure that animals are not fatigued or under stress and are adequately rested
- To condemn diseased animals that may pose public health risk
- To segregate suspected animals for detailed examination
- To examine the animals for toxic conditions and residues of drugs, antibiotics and pesticides
- To examine the cleanliness status of animals
- To identify injured animals or those with painful conditions for humane handling and emergency slaughter
- To report cases that require careful handling during slaughter and more critical post mortem inspection

## 11.3 Inspection facilities

- Adequate lairage space with feeding and watering facility
- Pens of appropriate size in sufficient numbers maintained in sanitary condition
- All pens, driveways and ramps to be free from sharp objects that may cause injury or pain to animals
- Well constructed floors to provide good footing for animals
- Restraining device for close examination and taking temperatures
- Sufficient lighting especially at the inspection point
- Separate pens for isolating suspect and condemned animals
- Veterinarian's office with personal facilities

- Adequate supporting staff trained to move, segregate, restrain, identify and dispose the animals

## 11.4 Principles of ante-mortem inspection

Animals should be inspected at rest and while in motion. Both sides of the animals should be examined.

The animal must be examined on the day of arrival at the abattoir.

Ante-mortem inspection should be carried out within 24 hours prior to slaughter. If slaughter is delayed more than 24 hours, it should be repeated.

Feverish animal should be segregated till the fever subsides without medication. Clinical samples may be taken where diagnosis requires laboratory confirmation. Such animals should be subjected to repeat ante-mortem inspection once the fever subsides or favourable laboratory report is obtained. However, animals with high grade fever may require condemnation due to the possibility of septicaemia.

Sick or suspect animals, and those in poor condition should be adequately identified and marked by recording species, class, age, condition, colour and markings. Special attention must be paid to the animals requiring casualty and emergency slaughter so that they do not pose health risk to abattoir workers and meat consumers subsequently.

Females in oestrus, aggressive animals, and horned animals should be isolated to prevent fighting and injury.

## 11.5 Abnormal conditions

In general, ante-mortem inspection should be carried out to segregate normal healthy animals from abnormal and unhealthy animals. Therefore, any animal that deviates from normal should be segregated during the initial screening process. Some possible abnormalities that can be helpful in screening out suspect animals are given below.

- Poor general appearance, emaciation, undernourished, immature, pregnant and high fever
- Abnormalities in respiration rate, coughing and difficulty in breathing
- Abnormalities in behaviour, walking in circles, pushing head against a wall, charging at various objects, aggression, dull and anxious expression in the eyes
- Abnormal gait due to pain in the legs, chest or abdomen or nervous disease
- Abnormal posture such as tucked up abdomen, head lowered and extended and stretched out feet
- Abnormalities in structure (conformation) such as swellings (abscesses), enlarged joints, umbilical swelling, hernia, enlarged mastitic udder, lumpy jaw and bloated abdomen
- Abnormal growth of tissues, tumours
- Abnormal discharge from the nose, excessive saliva from the mouth, bloody diarrhoea and protrusions from the natural orifices such as prolapsed rectum and uterus
- Abnormal colour such as black areas on horses and swine, red areas on light coloured skin (inflammation), dark blue areas on the skin or udder suggestive of gangrene
- Inadequate cleanliness
- Abnormal odour due to opening of an abscess, recent medication, ingestion of stinkweed or an acetone odour of ketosis
- Recumbency

## 11.6 Judgement on ante-mortem inspection

After completing the task of ante-mortem inspection, veterinary officer passes judgement regarding the condition of each animal. The animals are put in any one of the following categories.

### *Passed for slaughter*

These are animals that have been judged normal and apparently healthy and so can proceed to slaughter without undue delay.

### *Passed for slaughter subject to a second ante-mortem inspection after an additional holding period*

Animals that would fall in this category include those that have been insufficiently rested, or are temporarily affected by a condition that may be contrary to public health. In such cases a second ante-mortem inspection should be carried out after an additional holding period.

### *Passed for slaughter under special conditions*

Where it is suspectd that postmortem inspection findings could result in partial or total condemnation, the animals are treated as suspects. Their slaughter is deferred, preferably to the end of normal slaughter process of the day so that contamination of good quality carcasses is prevented.

### *Condemned animals*

The animals that are likely to pose meat-borne hazards, occupational health hazards or the likelihood of unacceptable contamination of the slaughter and dressing environment following slaughter are put in the condemned category and are promptly isolated and declared unfit for slaughter. The animals may also be condemned due to meat suitability reasons or animal health reasons.

### *Emergency slaughter*

This judgement is made when an animal is in acute pain or is suffering from a condition where a delay in slaughter would be contrary to animal welfare and that the delay could deteriorate the animal's condition. It should critically be ensured that slaughter of such animal should not present any hazard to the consumer. The cases of fractures, severe injuries, uterine prolapse and post-partum uterine haemorrhages in the bovine can be included in this category after critical ante-mortem inspection to rule out any other serious disease.

## 11.7 Ante-mortem inspection procedure in poultry

The birds are generally brought in crates to the poultry processing plants. It is, therefore, difficult to carry out thorough ante-mortem inspection of individual birds that arrive in very large number.

Hence, it may be advisable to conduct the health inspection of the birds by the veterinary officer of the concerned poultry farm who should issue a certificate regarding fitness of birds for slaughter. The certificate should be sent to the poultry processing plant alongwith the birds. In case of small farmers, the producer should sent the details of the birds alongwith a declaration regarding fitness for slaughter.

At poultry processing plant, the following procedure may be adopted.

Inspect the record and certificate sent by the producer.

Conduct superficial inspection of the general condition of the birds.

Segregate the birds showing abnormal behaviour, signs of disease or suffering from a transmissible disease.

Remove the birds that have arrived dead.

Examine individual birds after these have been shackled.

**Record sheet -** Ante-mortem inspection of food animals

| Animal identification | Species and sex of the animal | Time and date of ante-mortem inspection | Clinical signs and body temperature | Judgement | Reasons for holding from slaughter |
|---|---|---|---|---|---|
| | | | | | |
| | | | | | |
| | | | | | |
| | | | | | |
| | | | | | |
| | | | | | |
| | | | | | |
| | | | | | |
| | | | | | |
| | | | | | |

Module 12

# Components of a modern abattoir

An abattoir is essentially a food factory and therefore, its design and operation implies all the elements essential with respect to food hygiene. This is mostly related with materials used in construction, facilities for separation and storage of edible and inedible products, and cleaning. It is well known that the food animal is a reservoir of microorganisms which are present on the skin and in the gut, whereas meat from a healthy animal is generally considered to be practically sterile. Therefore, in the construction of modern abattoirs, the concept of dirty and clean areas of the plant is well addressed by keeping these two areas separate and at the best possible distance. The modern abattoir has following components.

## 12.1 Lairage

## 12.2 Slaughter hall

## 12. 3 Emergency slaughter room

12. 4 Refrigeration room

12. 5 Detained meat room

12. 6 Condemned meat room

12.7 Hide and skin store

12. 8 Gut and tripe room

12. 9 Offal room

12.10 Edible fat holding room

12.11 Cutting rooms

## 12.12 Equipment wash area

## 12.13 Meat dispatch area

## 12.14 Manure bay

## 12.15 Vehicle washing area

## 12.16 Facilities for personnel

## 12.17 Veterinary office

## 12.18 Laboratory

## 12.19 Effluent treatment plant

**Record sheet -** Layout of abattoir

**Record sheet -** Layout of slaughter hall

Module 13

# Procedure of slaughter and dressing

The modern methods of slaughter of meat animals are aimed at increasing production rate as well as carrying out the entire operation in a scientific manner to ensure humane conditions to minimize cruelty and pain to the animal. Modern slaughterhouses are equipped with automated carcass dressing line system that aids in hygienic meat production.

The major objectives of hygienic slaughter are:

- To produce safe meat of high quality
- To prevent contamination of the edible portions of the carcass with soiling material from the hides, skins and pelts, and from the contents of the internal organs
- To inhibit microbial growth on the surfaces of carcasses or meat
- To remove any carcasses or portions of carcass that are deemed unsuitable for human consumption

In modern abattoir, on-the-rail dressing system is adopted, wherein, the carcass is conveyed along an overhead rail, either by gravity or by electric power.

After stunning, the animal is shackled and hoisted on the overhead rail. The subsequent process is divided into different stages. When the carcass reaches an operator, he carries out his part of the process and sends the carcass to the next operator.

Different stages of the slaughter process in different kinds of animals are shown in the flow diagrams.

## 13.1 Procedure of slaughter and dressing of cattle/buffaloes

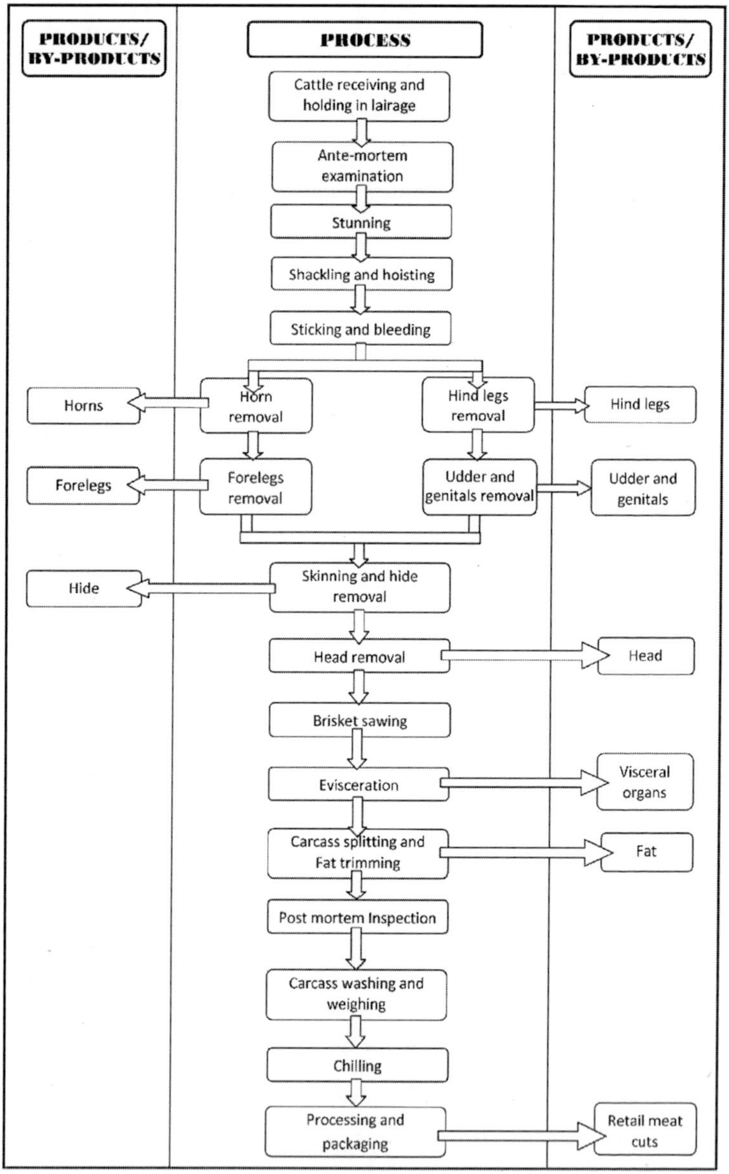

## 13.2 Procedure of slaughter and dressing of sheep/goats

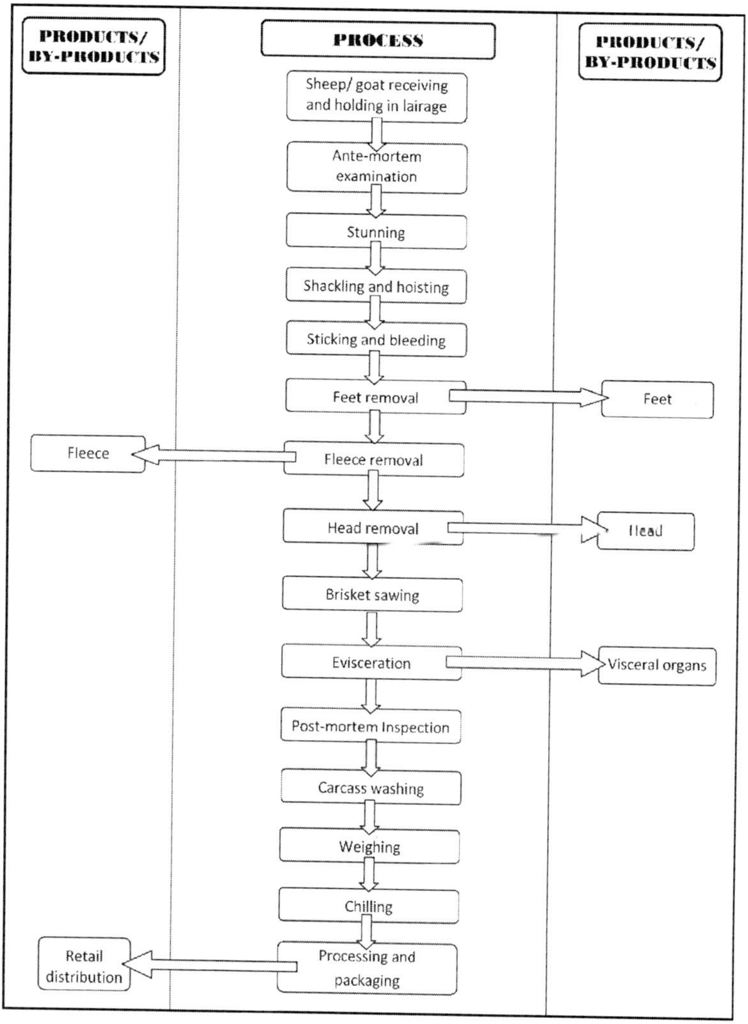

## 13.3 Procedure of slaughter and dressing of pigs

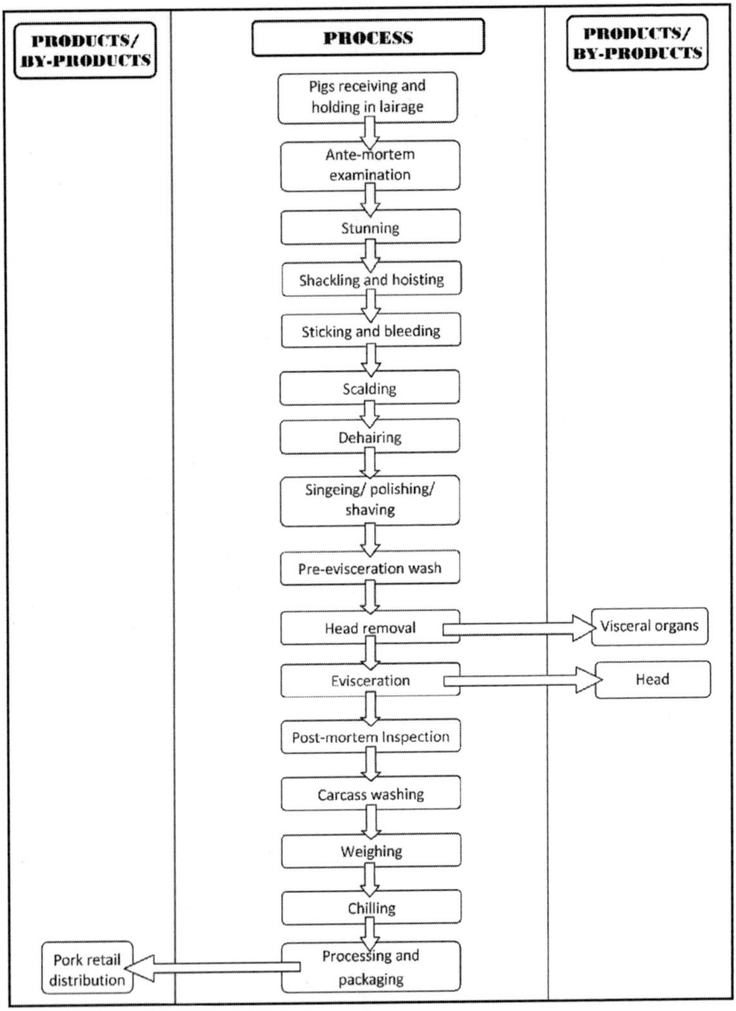

## 13.4 Procedure of slaughter and dressing of poultry

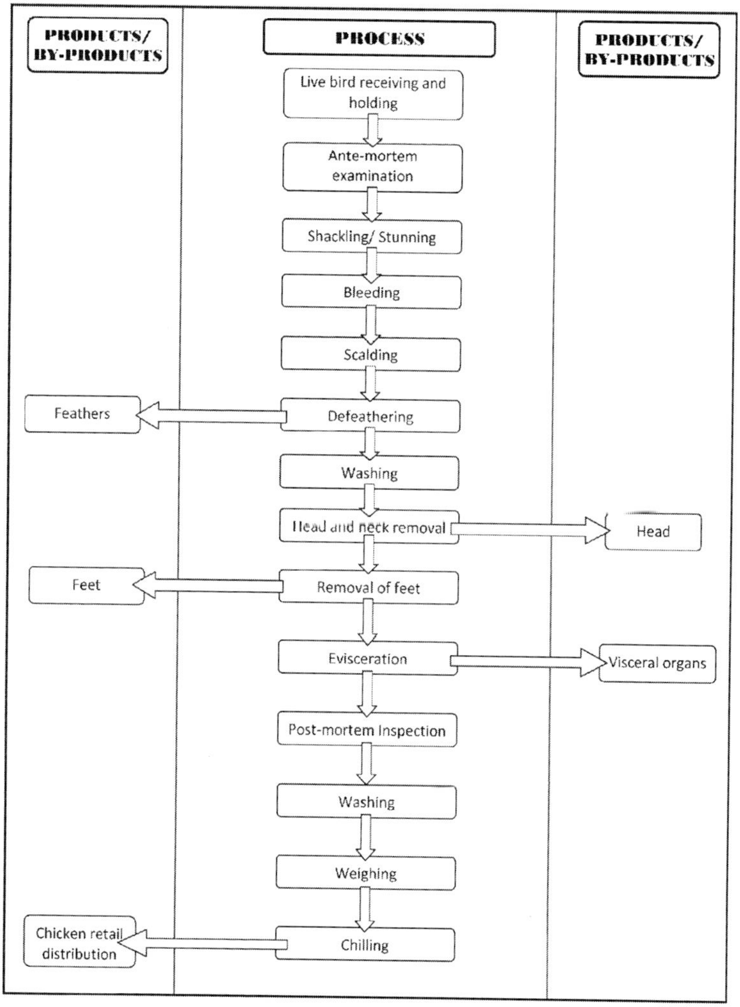

## Record sheet

### Stunning procedure in the abattoir

### Site of application of percussive stunning

## Record sheet

### Slaughter procedure in the abattoir

Module 14

# Post-mortem inspection of animals in abattoir

The post-mortem inspection is carried out to ensure that the meat produced is wholesome, disease-free, hygienic and safe to consumers. Post-mortem inspection requires skills of observation and evaluation and also takes into consideration the findings of ante-mortem inspection as well as any other information on the disease history of the herd or region of origin of the animals.

## 14.1 Purpose of post-mortem inspection

- Detection and elimination of meat that is affected with disease or contamination
- Certification regarding whether or not the meat is fit for human consumption
- Evaluation of efficiency of bleeding and slaughter and dressing techniques
- Separation of inferior quality meat and conditionally fit meat
- Collection of data on disease prevalence for feed back to the origin of the animals

## 14.2 Post-mortem inspection facilities

- Structural and mechanical facilities for efficient and comfortable working conditions

- Provision of presenting carcass, viscera and other parts of an individual animal in a synchronized way to the veterinary inspector
- Adequate diffused lighting at the inspection point for showing colours of the material without distortion
- Adequate facilities for personal hygiene, hand washing units with running hot and cold water, liquid soap, towels etc.
- Hot water sterilizers at the inspection table for disinfection of post-mortem instruments
- Data recording system

## 14.3 General principles of post-mortem inspection

Post-mortem inspection should be carried out in a systematic manner by a trained person.

Post-mortem inspection should be carried out immediately after dressing.

Each and every animal should undergo post-mortem inspection.

No part of the animal including organs not intended for human consumption should be removed and disposed until post-mortem inspection is complete.

If blood is collected for human consumption, it should be subjected to inspection.

## 14.4 Basic steps in post-mortem inspection

The post-mortem inspection involves the following.

- Visual examination of the whole carcass and organs
- Palpation of organs
- Incision of organs/ tissues
- Classification of lesions/ conditions into acute or chronic stages

- Establishing whether the condition is localized or generalized
- Determining the relation of lesions to diseases
- Coordinating the findings of ante-mortem and post-mortem inspection for final diagnosis
- Retaining suspected meat and other material awaiting laboratory report, final diagnosis and judgement
- Recording observations
- Stamping the carcass and offals regarding fitness for consumption
- Disposal of condemned carcasses and material

## 14.5 Post-mortem inspection procedure

The post-mortem inspection of individual organs and carcass should be carried out in a systematic manner in which all parts including head and viscera of carcasses are examined. Special attention should be given to the species specific conditions and diseases.

### 14.5.1 Bovines above 6 months age

#### *Head*

- Visual inspection of the outer surface
- Eyes for abnormal appearance or colour e.g. yellowing indicating icterus
- Mandible for irregular shape e.g. in actinobacillosis
- Gums, lips, tongue for signs of foot and mouth disease, stomatitis, actinomycosis, actinobacillosis
- Palpation of tongue for actinobacillosis etc.
- Examination of cheek muscles for *Cysticercus bovis* cysts by giving two parallel incisions in the external cheek muscles and one cut in the internal cheek muscles
- Examination by palpation and incision of retropharyngeal, submaxillary and parotid lymph nodes for abscesses, tuberculosis etc.

### *Lungs*

- Visual inspection and palpation for pneumonia, hydatid cysts, abscesses, tumours etc.
- Incision of bronchial and mediastinal lymph nodes to detect tuberculosis
- Incision to open trachea and bronchi to examine for inflammation, parasites, foreign bodies etc.

### *Heart*

- Visual inspection of the pericardium for pericarditis and haemorrhages etc.
- Inspection of amount and appearance of fluid by opening pericardial sac
- Incision to open all chambers to examine for endocarditis, *Cysticercus bovis* cysts

### *Liver*

- Visual examination and palpation for detecting degenerations, dystrophies, abscesses, hydatid cysts, tumours, tuberculosis lesions and liver flukes
- Palpation and incision of hepatic lymph nodes for any disease signs
- Incision of bile duct for liver fluke infestation

### *Spleen*

- Visual inspection for colour and size, dark color and enlargement suggesting infectious diseases and septicaemia

### *Alimentary tract*

- Visual inspection of rumen and intestine for enteritis etc.
- Palpation of mesenteric lymph nodes and incision, if required
- Palpation of oesophagus for parasitic cysts etc.

### *Kidneys*

- Visual inspection and palpation

- Incision of renal lymph nodes, if abnormalities detected

*Uterus*

- Visual inspection and palpation
- Incision only if any abnormality detected

*Udder*

- Visual inspection and palpation for abscesses, mastitis and tuberculosis

*Carcass*

- Visual examination of carcass (including musculature, exposed bones, joints, tendon sheaths etc.) for any signs of disease or defect
- Examination of bodily condition, efficiency of bleeding, colour, condition of serous membranes (pleura and peritoneum), cleanliness and the presence of any unusual odours
- Examination of muscle tissues for bruising
- Examination of superficial inguinal, external and internal iliac, prepectoral and renal lymph nodes
- Inspection of abdominal cavity for signs of adherence (peritonitis)
- Inspection of thoracic cavity for signs of pleurisy, tuberculosis etc.
- If necessary, incision of muscles for parasitic cysts, avoiding unnecessary cuts

### 14.5.2 Calves (less than 6 months)

Inspection procedure similar as for adult bovine animals

Particular attention to umbilical region and joints for inflammations which may be due to salmonellosis

Incision of cheek muscles, liver etc. for parasites may not be required

### 14.5.3 Sheep and goats

Inspection procedure similar as for adult bovine animals

Inspection largely based on visual inspection and palpation

Visual inspection and palpation of lungs for hydatid cysts, nematodes etc.

Visual inspection and palpation of liver for liver fluke

Incision of bile duct for presence of liver fluke

### 14.5.4 Pigs

Inspection procedure similar to bovines over 6 months

Careful visual inspection for any skin lesions e.g. swine erysipelas, swine fever, shotty eruptions and urticaria

Visual inspection and palpation of blade of the tongue for *Cysticercus cellulosae* cysts

Incision and inspection of submaxillary lymph nodes for tuberculosis

Incision of muscles of mastication, abdominal muscles, diaphragmatic muscles and root of the tongue for *Cysticercus cellulosae* cysts.

Collection of muscle sample from the root of the diaphragm for laboratory inspection for *Trichinella* infection

### 14.5.5 Poultry

Inspection of carcasses as well as viscera

Inspection for external lesions on the carcass e.g. swelling of sinuses, nasal and ocular discharges (if head is present), skin lesions, joint swellings etc.

Visual inspection of carcass for air sac inflammations, peritonitis, oviduct inflammation etc.

Visual inspection for contamination by faecal matter and bile

Visual inspection and palpation of intestinal tract, liver, spleen and heart

## 14.6 Decisions at the post-mortem examination

### 14.6.1 Approved, safe and suitable for human consumption

If the carcass and its associated offal are free from any evidence of disease or other abnormality, they are passed as fit for human consumption and stamped accordingly.

### 14.6.2 Condemned, totally unfit for human consumption

A number of diseases or conditions make it necessary to declare the unfit for human consumption. A list of such diseases is given in Table 14.1. These include many zoonotic diseases. The material affected with nonzoonotic diseases is condemned to prevent spread of animal diseases through food chain.

### 14.6.3 Partially condemned, partially fit for human consumption

When a disease or condition is localized in some parts or organs while the remaining portion does not carry any risk of disease transmission, only the affected portion or organ is removed, declared condemned and disposed of. The remaining parts are passed for human consumption. A list of such conditions is given in Table 14.2.

### 14.6.4 Conditionally fit for human consumption

A carcass or organ is considered conditionally fit for human consumption which in some way may be hazardous for human health. It is necessary to give a prescribed treatment to conditionally fit meat to make it safe for consumption. e.g. by cooking or freezing

Hygienically unsatisfactory meat and meat having few *Cysticercus* cysts may fall in this category which can be made safe by heat processing.

### 14.6.5 Inferior meat

The meat which has some minor deviations from the wholesome quality but does not present any health risk, it may be categorized as inferior or lower grade meat and marked accordingly for distribution at lower prices from special counters.

### 14.6.6 Fit for human consumption with distribution restrictions to a limited geographic area for animal health reasons

When the meat is affected with a particular disease or infection that does not make it fit for human consumption, it may be passed fit for distribution in a restricted area only where the infection in animals already exists. Such meat is restricted from going to other area where the disease is not prevalent to prevent its spread.

**Table 14.1 Diseases and conditions that necessitate total condemnation of carcass and viscera**

| Animals |
|---|
| African horse sickness |
| Anthrax |
| Blue tongue (severe cases) |
| Bovine malignant catarrhal fever (when disease is in advanced stage) |
| Bovine viral diorrhoea (acute form of disease) |
| Brucellosis |
| Campylobacteriosis |
| Caseous lymphadenitis (generalized condition) |
| Clostridial diseases such as bacillary haemoglobinurea, black quarter, botulism, braxy, tetanus, colibacillosis |
| Contagious ecthyma (severe cases) |
| Foot and mouth disease |
| Glanders |
| Johne's disease (in case of emaciated carcass) |
| Listeriosis |
| Pneumonic pasteurellosis (in early stage of disease) |
| Tularemia |
| Haemorrhagic septicaemia |
| Pox disease (in acute cases) |
| Pseudorabies/ Aujeszky's disease (when lesions are widespread) |
| Rabies |
| Rift valley fever |
| Rinderpest (in case of febrile and toxaemic state) |
| Salmonellosis |
| Scrapie |
| Swine erysipelas (in case of septicemic form) |
| Tuberculosis (when lesions are generalized, lesions present in bone joints and lymph nodes, history of fever on ante-mortem examination, associated cachexia) |
| Cysticercosis (generaised condition) |

| Trichinosis |
|---|
| Fascioliasis (if icterus is present) |
| Paraamphistomiasis ((in case of systemic changes) |
| Toxoplasmosis (in case of acute cases) |
| Trypanosomiasis (in case of acute cases) |
| Hypomagnesaemic tetany |
| Pregnancy toxaemia |
| Parturient paresis/milk fever |
| Porcine stress syndrome (depending on severity of condition) |
| Fever |
| Improper bleeding |
| Neoplasm (depending on severity of condition) |
| **Poultry** |
| Air sacculitis |
| Ascitis or dropsy |
| Chlamydiosis |
| Fowl typhoid |
| Pasteurellosis (in case of septicemia carcass) |
| Pseudotuberculosis (in case of generalized condition) |
| Pullorum disease |
| Tuberculosis |
| Lymphoid leukosis |
| Myeloid leukosis |
| Erythroid leukosis |
| Marek's disease |
| New castle disease |
| Gumboro |
| Coccidiosis (in case of emaciated or edematous conditions) |
| Aspergillosis |

***Source***: Govindrajalu M (2004) Post-mortem inspection. In: Textbook of Elements of Veterinary Public Health. Sherikar AT, Bachhil VN and Thapliyal DC (Eds.) Indian Council of Agricultural Research, New Delhi.

**Table 14.2 Diseases and conditions that necessitate only partial condemnation of carcass and viscera**

| **Disease** | **Organs/ body parts of major concern** |
|---|---|
| **Animals** | |
| Actinobacillosis | Head |
| Actinomycois | Head |
| Adenomatosis | Lung |
| Blue tongue (in less severe cases) | Mouth |
| Atrophic rhinitis | Head |
| Bovine malignant catarrhal fever (in early stage of disease progression) | Lungs, head |
| Bovine viral diorrhoea (in case of chronic status) | Alimentary tract |
| Brucellosis (depending upon local incidence and economics, carcass may be passed after heat treatment) | Reproductive system |
| Caseous lymphadenitis (localised condition) | Affected lymph node and its associated organs |
| Contagious bovine pleuropneumonia (CBPP) | Lungs and pleural adhesions |
| Contagious caprine pluropneumonia (CCPP) | Lungs and pleural adhesions |
| Contagious ecthyma (mild cases) | Head |
| Foot and mount disease (carcass may be passed after heat treatment) | Head, feet, udder |
| Johne's disease (when carcass is not emaciated) | Viscera and lymph nodes |
| Necrobacillosis | Rumen and liver |
| Pneumonic pasteurellosis (in case of chronic cases) | Lungs |
| Pox disease (recovered cases) | Skin |
| Pseudorabies/ Aujeszky's disease (recovered cases) | Skin, lungs, spleen, liver |
| Rift valley fever (recovered cases) | Heart, liver, spleen, |

| | |
|---|---|
| | alimentary tract |
| Rinderpest | Alimentary tract |
| Swine erysipelas (iIn case of urticarial form) | Skin, spleen, lymph nodes |
| Tuberculosis (when TB lesions are not so severe, carcass may be passed after heat treatment) | Lungs and all other internal organs |
| Ringworm | Skin |
| Hydatidosis | Removal of affected organ/part |
| Ascaris | Intestine |
| Pimply gut | Intestine |
| Kidney worm | Affected organ/ tissue |
| Thorny headed worms of pigs | Intestine |
| Lung worms | Lung and related organs |
| Fascioliasis (in absence of icterus) | Liver |
| Paramphistomiasis ((in absence of anemia or any other systemic changes) | Rumen |
| Blood flukes | Liver |
| Coccidiosis | Intestine, liver |
| Warble flies | Skin, oesophagus |
| Sheep nostril fly | Head |
| Photosensitization | Skin |
| Neoplasm (after removal of affected part) | Any affected part/ organ |
| **Poultry** | |
| Pasterurellosis (in absence of septicaemic condition) | Head |
| Histomoniasis | Liver and gut |

***Source***: Govindrajalu M (2004) Post-mortem inspection. In: Textbook of Elements of Veterinary Public Health. Sherikar AT, Bachhil VN and Thapliyal DC (Eds.) Indian Council of Agricultural Research, New Delhi.

## **Record sheet -** Lymph node inspection

### Cattle carcass

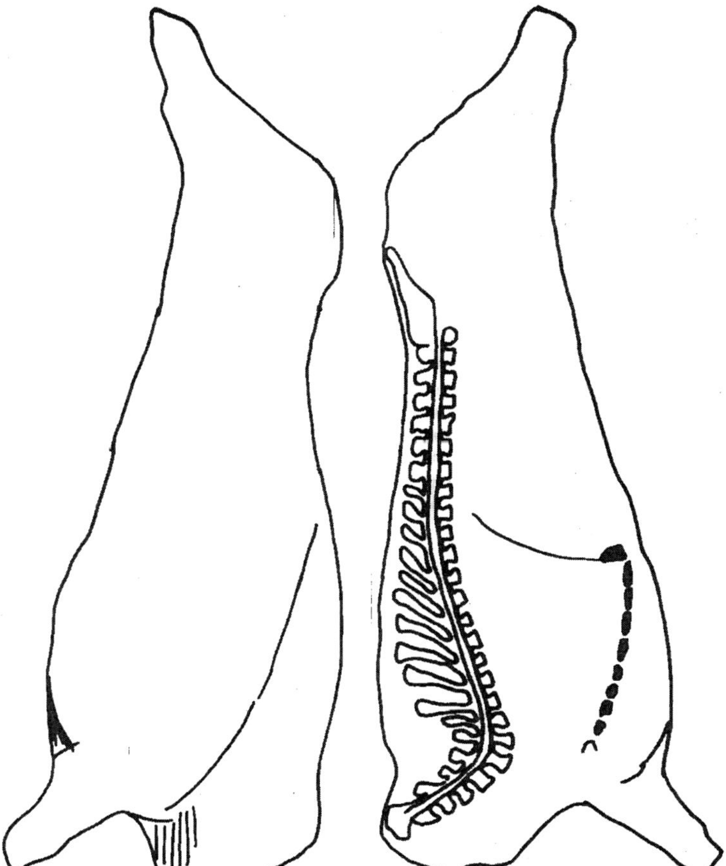

**Lateral side** **Medial side**

**Sheep carcass**

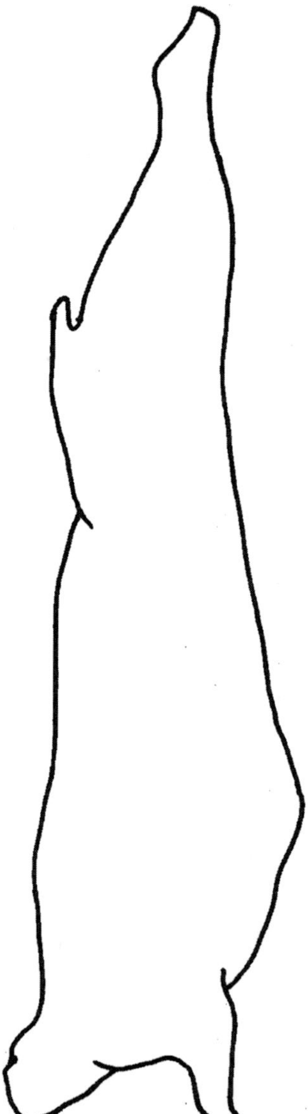

**Pig carcass**

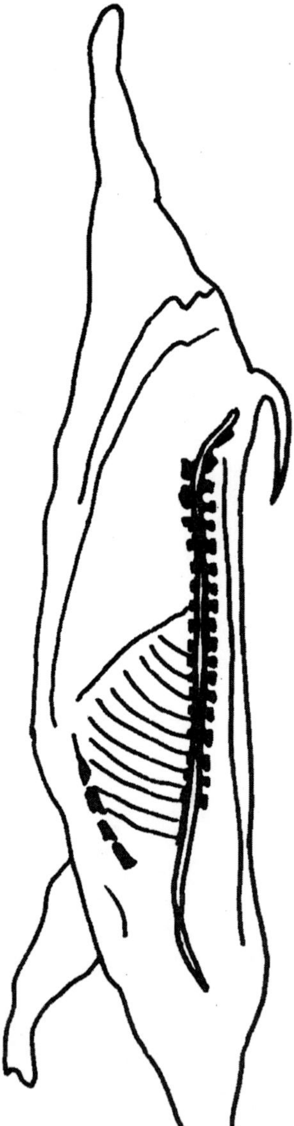

**Record sheet -** Post-mortem inspection of animals in abattoir

| Animal identification | Species and sex of the animal | Lesions | Diagnosis | Judgement | Reasons for judgement |
|---|---|---|---|---|---|
| | | | | | |
| | | | | | |
| | | | | | |
| | | | | | |
| | | | | | |
| | | | | | |
| | | | | | |
| | | | | | |
| | | | | | |
| | | | | | |

Module 15

# Sampling of meat and meat products

Sampling constitutes collection of a small portion of a larger amount for examination. For accurate results, it is quite important that the sample be as representative as possible of the whole lot of the material intended to be examined. Sampling, therefore, is not simply collecting a small portion from the lot, but requires systematic planning, scientific procedure, specialized equipment and trained personnel.

The sampling of carcasses and meat can be done either by collecting superficial samples or deep samples or both depending upon the requirement of the tests to be carried out.

## 15.1 Collection of superficial samples

Superficial samples are taken to assess the level of surface contamination present on the carcass or meat. Sampling can be done by swab method, rinse method, contact method, or collecting thin slices from the surface.

### 15.1.1 Swab method

- Take a sterile thin metallic template of a measured area and hold over the carcass or meat portion.
- Take a sterile non-absorbent cotton wool swab and moisten it in sterile physiological saline.
- Rub the swab over the test surface area first in one direction and then at right angle to it, frequently turning the swab.
- Put the swab in a sterile test tube.
- Add 10 ml of diluent or physiological saline and shake very well.

- Use the sample for microbiological analysis and calculate the microbial load per square cm of the sampled area.

### 15.1.2 Rinse method (useful for small items)

- Take the material to be examined and wash in a known volume of normal saline solution by rinsing.
- Use the suspension for analysis.

### 15.1.3 Contact method

- Use agar medium surface contact or impression plate.
- Press it against the test surface to collect the surface microorganisms.
- Cover the plate with lid and proceed for incubation directly.

### 15.1.4 Surface slice method

- Remove thin slices from the surface with sterile scalpels and forceps.
- Weigh the sample.
- Homogenize the sample in known volume of normal saline solution and use for analysis.

## 15.2 Collection of deep samples

- Collect deep samples of meat with sterile scalpels and forceps, avoiding contamination from the surface.
- Weigh the sample and use for analysis.

## 15.3 Collection of sample from packaged food

- Collect the samples of packaged, processed or canned meat according to a recommended sampling plan. The sampling plan for a product includes the following attributes:

  n = number of samples to be taken from the lot

  c = number of samples permitted to fail

  m = microbial count below which the sample is considered satisfactory

M = microbial count above which the sample is considered unsatisfactory

Module 16

# Examination of physical quality of meat

The physical quality of meat influences its acceptance by the consumers. Physical quality of meat is attributed to physical characteristics such as colour, odour, texture and finish. Measurement of extract release volume and water holding capacity of meat also help in detection of spoilage and evaluation of physical quality of meat.

## 16.1 Physical examination of meat for quality assurance

Observe the meat for colour, texture and finish.

The meat appears dark and sticky shortly after slaughter. On squeezing, it releases water with great difficulty. After a day or so i.e. after adequate rigor mortis, the meat is lighter in colour. The meat is moist but not sticky and 30% of fluid can be squeezed from it.

The normal colour of beef and buffalo meat is bright to dark red but in case of meat of old animals of over 3 years age, the colour is dark red.

The colour of sheep meat is light pink to dark pink and that of goat is dark pink.

Pig meat is grayish pink while poultry meat is whitish. Rabbit meat is bright red with bluish sheen.

Observe the meat for dark, firm and dry (DFD) condition. The meat may appear dark, firm and dry where the freshly slaughtered carcass is darker and drier than normal. It occurs due to poor rigor mortis in case of exhausted or stressed animals, most commonly in cattle. The colour and flavour of DFD meat is less acceptable while the keeping quality of such meat is also lower.

In case of pork, observe the meat for pale, soft, exudative (PSE) muscle condition (watery pork) wherein flesh becomes pale and unattractive in colour and lacks flavour. It causes drip and weight loss. The condition is undesirable.

## 16.2 Determination of extract release volume (ERV)

The extract release volume is a valuable tool in determining incipient spoilage in meat as well as predicting the refrigerator shelf-life of meat. The test assesses the amount of aqueous extract released from a slurry of meat when allowed to pass through filter paper for a given period of time. Fresh beef of good organoleptic quality with a relatively low bacterial number releases large volume of extract (high ERV), whereas beef in the process of microbial spoilage with a high bacterial number releases less extract (less ERV) or none.

### 16.2.1 Materials

| | | |
|---|---|---|
| Meat sample | 0.05 M PBS (pH 5.8) | Weighing balance |
| Petri dishes | Homogenizer | Beaker |
| Funnel | Whatman filter paper No. 1 | Measuring cylinder |
| pH paper | | |

### 16.2.2 Procedure

Take 15 g of minced meat sample and blend it with 60 ml of 0.05 M phosphate buffer saline (PBS, pH 5.8) in a tissue homogenizer for 2 minutes.

Put the meat slurry for filtration through Whatman filter paper No. 1 for 15 minutes.

Measure the volume of the filtrate (meat extract) collected in measuring cylinder within 15 minutes. The volume of extract is ERV.

### 16.2.3 Interpretation

Meat with an ERV above 25 ml is considered acceptable.

**Record sheet** - Determination of extract release volume

| Sample No. | Extract release volume | Interpretation |
|---|---|---|
| | | |
| | | |
| | | |
| | | |
| | | |

## 16.3 Determination of water holding capacity (WHC)

Water holding capacity is the ability of meat to retain its inherent moisture on application of external pressures like gravity, heating, centrifugation and pressing. It mainly depends on the degree of hydration of muscle protein and influences the appearance, texture, tenderness, juiciness and weight loss or shrinkage during cooking. Most of the water in muscles is present in myofibrils and in spaces between actin and myocin filaments. One part of hydration water of muscle is tightly bound, known as fixed bound hydration water or true hydration water. The other part of water is free water or loose water which can be immobilized on applying any force.

A beef of good organoleptic quality and low bacterial count has a low WHC (high free water on pressing) whereas microbiologically spoiled beef has a progressively higher WHC manifested by smaller free water. It is also influenced by other factors such as age and sex of animal, concentration of salts, stage of rigor and the pH of meat.

The measurement of WHC of meat can be carried out in different ways. Most of the methods of WHC estimation are based on measuring the water liberated by the muscle tissue on applying pressure. Filter paper press technique has been widely used which is very simple and rapid as described below.

### 16.3.1 Materials

| | | |
|---|---|---|
| Meat sample | Plexiglass plates | Forceps and scissors |
| Whatman filter paper No. 1 | Oven | Moisture balance |
| Weights | Electronic balance | |

### 16.3.2 Procedure

Take a portion of meat sample and process it for determining its moisture content. For this, weigh out a known amount of sample and air dry it in a hot air oven at 100-105➡C for 16-18 hours or till a constant weight is obtained. The difference between the weight of sample and dried sample provides the moisture content.

Take two sheets of Whatman filter paper and weigh them on electronic balance.

To determine WHC, take exactly 1 g finely ground meat sample and place it between the two previously weighed Whatman filter papers.

Place these filter papers along with meat sample between two plexiglass plates.

Press the plates with at least 18 Kg weight for one minute.

Remove the pressed meat film from the filter papers and weigh the wet filter papers on electronic balance.

Calculate the amount of free water by subtracting the weight of dry filter paper from the weight of wet filter paper.

Free water = weight of wet filter paper – weight of dry filter paper

Calculate the WHC from the following formula.

$$WHC = \frac{(\text{Total moisture content} - \text{Free water})}{\text{Total moisture content}} \times 100$$

### 16.3.3 Interpretation

The water holding capacity of meat of good organoleptic and bacteriological quality is low whereas high WHC indicates microbiological spoilage of meat. The WHC progressive increases with higher degree of spoilage. The normal range of WHC is 50-70% in meat of different kind of animals depending on the species of animal.

**Record sheet -** Determination of water holding capacity

| Sample No. | Observations | | WHC (%) | Interpretation |
|---|---|---|---|---|
| | Weight of sample kept for drying | | | |
| | Weight of sample after drying | | | |
| | Moisture content in meat | | | |
| | Dry filter paper weight | | | |
| | Wet filter paper weight | | | |
| | Free water content | | | |
| | Weight of sample kept for drying | | | |
| | Weight of sample after drying | | | |
| | Moisture content in meat | | | |
| | Dry filter paper weight | | | |
| | Wet filter paper weight | | | |
| | Free water content | | | |
| | Weight of sample kept for drying | | | |
| | Weight of sample after drying | | | |
| | Moisture content in meat | | | |
| | Dry filter paper weight | | | |
| | Wet filter paper weight | | | |
| | Free water content | | | |
| | Weight of sample kept for drying | | | |
| | Weight of sample after drying | | | |
| | Moisture content in meat | | | |
| | Dry filter paper weight | | | |
| | Wet filter paper weight | | | |
| | Free water content | | | |

Module 17

# Sensory evaluation of fish quality

Fish is a highly perishable product. The assessment of freshness and quality of fish is required at the landing sites, during processing, storage or prior to shipment. Inspection of fish may largely be carried out by visual, touch and olfactory observations. An experienced person can easily distinguish between good fish from poor quality fish by sensory methods.

The fish presented for inspection may be of the following types:

(a) Fresh fish

(b) Raw gutted fish stored in ice

(c) Raw gutted fish stored at ambient temperature (20-30→C)

## 17.1 Assessment of freshness of fish

Fresh fish should be examined for the following characteristics to distinguish between fresh fish and spoiled fish.

**Assessment of fish freshness**

| Character | Fresh fish | Spoiled fish |
|---|---|---|
| Odour | Light, desirable, characteristic of the water weeds | Undesirable, acrid, acid, putrid, ammonia-like |
| General aspect | Bright, iridescent pigmentation, no blood spots around the head, along the vertebral column | Dull pigmentation with no shine or reflections |
| Rigidity of the body | Rigid body, firm and elastic | Flaccid body, soft consistency. A slight pressure by the finger leaves a mark |

| Character | Fresh fish | Spoiled fish |
|---|---|---|
| Secretions | Humid fish, transparent mucus, no visible secretions | Presence of sticky secretions |
| Scales | Bright and firmly attached | Loosely bound and come out easily |
| Skin | Tight and adhering well | Wrinkled, discolored, easy to detach and cut |
| Eyes | Clear and bright pupil, convex (bulging), occupy all the orbital cavity, transparent | Dull opaque pupils, concave (shrunken), glassy, completely sunken |
| Gill-cover | Adheres firmly with no blood spots | Slightly detached with dark-red spots |
| Gills | Humid, shiny, pink or red | Dry, grayish or opaque |
| Abdomen | Neither swollen, saggy, tight or cut | Flaccid, deformed, often swollen, with dark blue, green or black spots |
| Anus | Tightly closed | Open, often prominent |
| Viscera | Smooth, clean, bright, nacreous, peritoneum sticks tightly to flesh | Sunken, swollen, fragile peritoneum |
| Vertebral column | Sticks firmly to muscles | Does not stick |
| Flesh | Firm and elastic, smooth surface, nacreous reflections | Soft, friable, red colored, especially along the vertebral column |

***Source:*** UNIDO (2011) Sensory methods for fish inspection and quality assurance. The United Nations Industrial Development Organization. http://www.unido.org

## 17.2 Assessment of raw gutted fish stored in ice

Fish stored in ice should be inspected by using the following scheme. Based on observations the fish can be catagorised into different grades and also given score.

**Assessment of raw, gutted fish stored in ice**

| **Character** | **Outer Appearance** | | | | | | |
|---|---|---|---|---|---|---|---|
| | **Skin** | **Gill color** | **Gill odour** | **Eyes** | **Texture** | **Grade** | **Score** |
| Freshness allowing distribution, if kept in ice | Natural brilliance, metallic, golden, pink-silver, scales firmly attached | Red-purple, maroon, no slime | Fresh, seaweedy | Transparent, yellow sheen | Firm, hard (rigor), elastic | 1st Quality | 9 |
| | | | | | | | 8 |
| | Brilliance, few dull patches, darkening, scales firm | Reddish, bleached patches, slime | Neutral, fresh, light, sourish | Reddish, yellow sheen | Firm, reduced elasticity | | 7 |
| | | | | | | | 6 |
| Reduced freshness, allowing for regional or local distribution if kept in ice | Dull, metallic patches, dark on dorsal side, yellow streaks on belly area, scales loose at belly area | Reddish with brown, bleached patches, slime | Light stinky, sweetish, sour, slightly rotten off-odors | Red, milky, turbid, flat | Soft | 2nd Quality | 5 |
| | | | | | | | 4 |
| Unfit for human consumption, sometimes limited consumption after frying | Dull, dark, yellow slime, scales loose | Reddish, brown, thick slime | Rotten, stinking, sulphidy, strong off-odors | Red, bloody, concave | Very soft, finger-prints leave impress-ions | Reject | 3 |
| | | | | | | | 2 |
| | | | | | | | 1 |

***Source***: UNIDO (2011) Sensory methods for fish inspection and quality assurance. The United Nations Industrial Development Organization. http://www.unido.org

## 17.3 Assessment of raw gutted fish stored at ambient temperature

The raw gutted fish stored at ambient temperature are inspected and evaluated on the basis of the feature given below in the Table.

**Assessment of raw, gutted fish stored at ambient temperature (20-30°C)**

| Character | Outer appearance | | | | | | |
|---|---|---|---|---|---|---|---|
| | **Skin** | **Gill color** | **Gill odor** | **Eyes** | **Texture** | **Grade** | **Score** |
| Freshness enabling limited local distribution | Natural brilliance, metallic, golden, pink-silver, scales firmly attached<br>Brilliance, few dull patches, scales firm | Red-purple, maroon, no slime<br>Reddish, little pinkish slime | Fresh, seaweedy<br>Neutral, fresh | Trans-parent, Yellow Sheen<br>Reddish, convex | Firm, hard (*rigor*), elastic<br>Firm, reduced elasticity | 1st Quality | 9<br>8<br>7<br>6 |
| Reduced freshness, allowing for quick sale<br>If preserved, local distribution | Grayish, darkening loss of metallic brightness<br>Scales loose on the belly | Bleached patches, slime | Light rotten off-odours | Red, milky, flat | Soft | 2nd. Quality | 5<br>4 |
| Unfit for human consumption, sometimes limited consumption after frying | Yellow slime, greenish fins, dull appearance, scales loose | Green, slime brown | Rotten, sour strong off-odours | Sunken, turbid | Soft, buttery, finger-prints leave impress-ions | Reject | 3<br>2<br>1 |

***Source***: UNIDO (2011) Sensory methods for fish inspection and quality assurance. The United Nations Industrial Development Organization. http://www.unido.org

**Record sheet** – Evaluation of fish quality

| Sample No. | Type of fish | Characteristics | Quality |
|---|---|---|---|
| | | | |
| | | | |
| | | | |
| | | | |
| | | | |
| | | | |
| | | | |

Module 18

# Hygienic quality assessment of meat and meat products

The internal tissues of healthy animal at the time of slaughter are generally considered to be free of bacteria, however, a variety of bacteria enter meat at different stages of slaughter and processing of meat from contaminated equipment, gastrointestinal tract and skin of animals, meat handlers and environment. Consequently, depending on the hygienic conditions, different types of bacteria in varying numbers are encountered in retail meat. These bacteria may cause spoilage of the products as well as may prove pathogenic to man. Hence, bacteriological examination of meat is very important for quality assurance and involves several tests. Standard plate count and coliform count tests are commonly employed to reflect the microbiological quality of foods in relation to shelf-life and safety.

## 18.1 Standard plate count test

The standard plate count (SPC) test is useful in assessing the bacterial load and helps in assessing the hygienic quality of meat and meat products and ultimately predicts their shelf-life.

### 18.1.1 Apparatus

| | | |
|---|---|---|
| Meat sample | Petri dishes | 1 ml and 10 ml pipettes |
| Conical flasks | Test tubes | Test tube stand |
| Water bath preset at 45°C | Incubator | Hot air oven |
| Autoclave | Colony counter | Burner |
| Marking pencil | | |

### 18.1.2 Culture medium and reagents

Plate count agar (see Section 4.2.2)

Normal saline solution (NSS) (see Section 4.2.2)

### 18.1.3 Procedure

Take 25 g meat sample aseptically and suspend in 225 ml NSS using a homogenizer, blender or pestle and mortar to make a uniform 1: 10 suspension of the sample.

Make further 10-fold dilutions from the 1:10 suspension in 9 ml NSS in tube.

Inoculate the diluted samples into the petri dishes and pour SPC agar (melted and held at 45-50➡C).

Mix properly and after solidification of agar incubate the plates at 37➡C.

### 18.1.4 Observations and recording of results

Observe the plates for colony forming units and record results as per the procedure given in Section 4.2.4.

The results are expressed as colony forming units per gram of meat (cfu/g).

### 18.1.5 Interpretation

The quality of different types of meat products and sea foods can be assessed on the basis of guidelines/ standards available for that product. The requirements prescribed in the Food Safety and Standards Regulations (2011) for meat and meat products are summarized in Table 18.1 and for sea foods in Table 18.2.

## 18.2 Coliform count test

Coliform bacteria include *Escherichia, Citrobacter, Enterobacter* and *Klebsiella* organisms of family Enterobacteriaceae. Coliform bacteria act as indicators of faecal contamination because these are normal inhabitants of intestine of warm-blooded animals. The presence of coliforms is suggestive of insanitary conditions during slaughter and processing of meat. Their count in meat and meat products helps in evaluation of hygienic quality of meat and meat products and indicates the possibility of pathogens in food.

### 18.2.1 Apparatus

| | | |
|---|---|---|
| Meat sample | Petri dishes | 1 ml and 10 ml pipettes |
| Conical flasks | Test tubes | Test tube stand |
| Water bath preset at 45°C | Incubator | Hot air oven |
| Autoclave | Colony counter | Burner |
| Marking pencil | | |

### 18.2.2 Culture medium/reagents

Violet red bile agar (VRBA) (See Section 4.5.2)

Normal saline solution (NSS) (See Section 4.2.2)

### 18.2.3 Procedure

Prepare 1:10 suspension of meat sample by suspending 25 g meat sample in 225 ml NSS aseptically,

Inoculate diluted sample in petri dishes.

Pour culture medium, mix and allow to solidify.

After solidification of the medium, pour another thin layer of VRBA (3-4 ml) to cover the entire surface of the previously solidified medium. Allow to solidify.

Incubate the plates at 37➡C for 24 hours as described in Section 4.5.3.

### 18.2.4 Observations and recording of results

Observe the plates for the appearance of characteristic colonies of coliform bacteria.

Coliforms give rise to purple-red coloured colonies with a zone of precipitation. The size of the colonies is 0.5 mm or more after 24 hours of incubation.

Count the cfu in appropriate dilution.

Calculate the number per g by multiplying with dilution factor.

### 18.2.5 Interpretation

The presence of large numbers of coliforms in foods is highly undesirable, however, it may not be practically possible to eliminate all coliforms from fresh and frozen meat. Therefore, in these food items only low number of coliform bacteria may be permissible dependent upon nature of the product and the type of processing it has undergone.

**Table 18.1 Microbiological requirements for meat and meat products as per Food Safety and Standards Regulations, 2011 (India)**

| Product | Total plate count | *Escherichia coli* | *Staphylococcus aureus* | *Clostridium perfringens* and *C. botulinum* |
|---|---|---|---|---|
| Canned corned beef | Max. 1000/g | Absent in 25 g | Absent in 25 g | Absent in 25 g |
| Canned luncheon meat | Max. 1000/g | Absent in 25 g | Absent in 25 g | Absent in 25 g |
| Canned cooked ham | Max. 1000/g | Absent in 25 g | Absent in 25 g | Absent in 25 g |
| Canned chopped meat | Max. 1000/g | Absent in 25 g | Absent in 25 g | Absent in 25 g |

| | | | | |
|---|---|---|---|---|
| Canned chicken | Max. 1000/g | Absent in 25 g | Absent in 25 g | Absent in 25 g |
| Canned mutton and goat meat | Max. 1000/g | Absent in 25 g | Absent in 25 g | Absent in 25 g |
| Frozen mutton, chicken, goat and buffalo meat | Max. 100000/g | Max. 100/g | Max. 100/g | Max. 30/g |

| **Product** | ***Salmonella*** | ***Listeria monocytogenes*** | **Yeast and mould count** |
|---|---|---|---|
| Canned corned beef | Absent in 25 g | | |
| Canned luncheon meat | Absent in 25 g | | |
| Canned cooked ham | Absent in 25 g | | |
| Canned chopped meat | Absent in 25 g | | |
| Canned chicken | Absent in 25 g | | |
| Canned mutton and goat meat | Absent in 25 g | | |
| Frozen mutton, chicken, goat and buffalo meat | Absent in 25 g | Absent in 25 g | Max. 1000/g |

**Table 18.2 Microbiological requirements for sea foods as per Food Safety and Standards Regulations, 2011 (India)**

| **Sr. No.** | **Name of the product** | **Total plate count** | ***Escherichia coli*** | ***Staphylococcus aureus*** | ***Salmonella & Shigella*** |
|---|---|---|---|---|---|
| 1. | Frozen shrimps or prawns | | | | |
| | Raw | Max. five lakhs/g | Max. 20/g | Max. 100/g | Absent in 25 g |
| | Cooked | Max. one lakh/g | Absent in 25 g | Absent in 25 g | Absent in 25 g |

| Sr. No. | Name of the product | Total plate count | *Escherichia coli* | *Staphylococcus aureus* | *Salmonella & Shigella* |
|---|---|---|---|---|---|
| 2. | Frozen lobsters | | | | |
| | Raw | Max. five lakhs/g | Max. 20/g | Max. 100/g | Absent in 25 g |
| | Cooked | Max. one lakh/g | Absent in 25 g | Absent in 25 g | Absent in 25 g |
| 3. | Frozen finfish | Max. five lakhs/g | Max. 20/g | Max. 100/g | Absent in 25 g |
| 4. | Frozen fish fillets or minced fish flesh or mixtures thereof | Max. five lakhs/g | Max. 20/g | Max. 100/g | Absent in 25 g |
| 5. | Dried shark fins | Max. five lakhs/g | Max. 20/g | Max. 100/g | Absent in 25 g |
| 6. | Salted fish/ dried salted fish | Max. five lakhs/g | Max. 20/g | Max. 100/g | Absent in 25 g |
| 7. | Canned finfish | Nil | Absent in 25 g | Absent in 25 g | Absent in 25 g |
| 8. | Canned shrimp | Nil | Absent in 25 g | Absent in 25 g | Absent in 25 g |
| 9. | Canned sardines or sardine type products | Nil | Absent in 25 g | Absent in 25 g | Absent in 25 g |
| 10. | Canned salmon | Nil | Absent in 25 g | Absent in 25 g | Absent in 25 g |
| 11. | Canned crab meat | Nil | Absent in 25 g | Absent in 25 g | Absent in 25 g |
| 12. | Canned tuna and bonito | Nil | Absent in 25 g | Absent in 25 g | Absent in 25 g |

**Table 18.2 continued**

| Sr. No. | Name of the product | *Vibrio cholerae* | *Vibrio parahaemolyticus* | *Clostridium perfringens* |
|---|---|---|---|---|
| 1. | Frozen shrimps or prawns | | | |
| | Raw | Absent in 25 g | Absent in 25 g | |
| | Cooked | Absent in 25 g | Absent in 25 g | |
| 2. | Frozen lobsters | | | |
| | Raw | Absent in 25 g | Absent in 25 g | |
| | Cooked | Absent in 25 g | Absent in 25 g | |
| 3. | Frozen fish, finfish | Absent in 25 g | Absent in 25 g | |
| 4. | Frozen fish fillets or minced fish flesh or mixtures thereof | Absent in 25 g | Absent in 25 g | |
| 5. | Dried shark fins | Absent in 25 g | Absent in 25 g | |
| 6. | Salted fish/ dried salted fish | Absent in 25 g | Absent in 25 g | |
| 7. | Canned finfish | Absent in 25 g | Absent in 25 g | Absent in 25 |
| 8. | Canned shrimp | Absent in 25 g | Absent in 25 g | |
| 9. | Canned sardines or sardine type products | Absent in 25 g<br>Absent in 25 g | Absent in 25 g | |
| 10. | Canned salmon | Absent in 25 g | Absent in 25 g | |
| 11. | Canned crab meat | Absent in 25 g | Absent in 25 g | |
| 12. | Canned tuna and bonito | Absent in 25 g | Absent in 25 g | |

**Record sheet -** Hygienic quality assessment of meat and meat products

| Sample No. and details | Parameter | Colony count | | | Dilution factor | cfu/g | Interpretation |
|---|---|---|---|---|---|---|---|
| | | Plate I | Plate II | Average | | | |
| | SPC | | | | | | |
| | Coliform | | | | | | |
| | SPC | | | | | | |
| | Coliform | | | | | | |
| | SPC | | | | | | |
| | Coliform | | | | | | |
| | SPC | | | | | | |
| | Coliform | | | | | | |
| | SPC | | | | | | |
| | Coliform | | | | | | |
| | SPC | | | | | | |
| | Coliform | | | | | | |
| | SPC | | | | | | |
| | Coliform | | | | | | |
| | SPC | | | | | | |
| | Coliform | | | | | | |

Module 19

# Examination of meat and meat products for pathogenic bacteria

A variety of pathogenic organisms originating from food animals, meat handlers and the environment may gain access to meat. The presence of these organisms, sometimes even in small numbers, may pose public health risk. It is therefore, quite essential that meat samples are examined to rule out their presence or establish that their numbers are below the permissible levels.

## 19.1 Detection of *Salmonella* in meat and meat products

*Salmonella* organisms are the most important among the Gram-negative bacteria that cause foodborne gastroenteritis. Food legislations of different countries generally demand to ensure that *Salmonella* is absent in meat and meat products, hence, examination of meat for *Salmonella* bears great significance.

### 19.1.1 Apparatus

Same as for milk product examination (Section 8.2.1)

### 19.1.2 Culture media/reagents

Same as for milk product examination (Section 8.2.2)

### 19.1.3 Procedure

Same as for milk product examination (Section 8.2.3)

### 19.1.4 Observations and recording of results

Same as for milk product examination (Section 8.2.4)

### 19.1.5 Interpretation

According to Food Safety and Standards Regulations (2011), *Salmonella* should be absent in 25 g of different kinds of meat products and sea foods. The details are given in Table 18.1 and 18.2.

**Record sheet -** Detection of *Salmonella* in meat and meat products

| Sample details | Isolate No. | Colony characteristics | Gram's reaction (-) | Reaction on TSI agar | $H_2S$ in TSI agar | Motility (+) | Lysine decarboxylase (+) | Nitrate reduction (-) | Indole (-) | Methyl red (+) | VP (-) | Urease (-) | Malonate (-) | Polyvalent O antiserum (+) | Polyvalent H antiserum (+) | Interpretation |
|---|---|---|---|---|---|---|---|---|---|---|---|---|---|---|---|---|
| | | | | | | | | | | | | | | | | |
| | | | | | | | | | | | | | | | | |
| | | | | | | | | | | | | | | | | |
| | | | | | | | | | | | | | | | | |
| | | | | | | | | | | | | | | | | |
| | | | | | | | | | | | | | | | | |
| | | | | | | | | | | | | | | | | |
| | | | | | | | | | | | | | | | | |
| | | | | | | | | | | | | | | | | |
| | | | | | | | | | | | | | | | | |

***Note***: Reactions of typical *Salmonella* are shown in parenthesis, - negative, + positive

## 19.2 Detection of *Listeria* in meat and meat products

*Listeria* is a Gram-positive organism which is widely distributed in nature. Among *Listeria, Listeria monocytogenes* is the most important species from public health point of view. Though the occurrence of foodborne listeriosis is less, the severity of listeriosis may be quite high leading to high fatality rate.

### 19.2.1 Apparatus

| | | |
|---|---|---|
| Conical flasks | Test tubes | Petri dishes |
| Pipettes | Inoculation loop | Marking pen |
| Bunsen burner | Incubator | |

### 19.2.2 Culture media/reagents

### (a) University of Vermont medium- I (UVM-I)

| | | |
|---|---|---|
| Proteose peptone | : | 5 g |
| Tryptone | : | 5 g |
| Yeast extract | : | 5 g |
| Lab Lamco | : | 5 g |
| Sodium chloride | : | 20 g |
| Di-sodium hydrogen phosphate | : | 12 g |
| Potassium di-hydrogen phosphate | : | 1.35 g |

Suspend the above ingredients in 960 ml distilled purified water. Mix thoroughly and adjust the pH to 7.4. Autoclave at 121°C for 15 minutes. After cooling the medium to 45°C, add the following constituents that are previously sterilized by filtration.

| | | |
|---|---|---|
| Esculin | : | 1g |
| Nalidixic acid | : | 40 mg |
| Acriflavine | : | 12 mg |

### (b) University of Vermont medium-II (UVM-II)

The composition is similar to UVM-I except that the amount of acriflavine is 25 mg per liter.

### (c) Oxford medium

(i) Oxford medium base

| | | |
|---|---|---|
| Pancreatic digest of casein | : | 8.9 g |
| Proteose peptone No. 3 | : | 4.4 g |
| Yeast extract | : | 4.4 g |
| Tryptic digest of beef heart | : | 2.7 g |
| Starch | : | 0.9 g |
| Sodium chloride | : | 4.4 g |
| Esculin | : | 1 g |
| Ferric ammonium citrate | : | 0.5 g |
| Lithium chloride | : | 15 g |
| Agar agar | : | 15.3 g |

Suspend all the above ingredients in 1 L of distilled water and mix thoroughly. Heat with frequent agitation and boil for 1 minute to completely dissolve the ingredients. Autoclave at 121°C for 10 minutes and allow to cool the base medium to 45-50°C.

(ii) Oxford medium antimicrobial supplement

| | | |
|---|---|---|
| Acriflavine | : | 5 mg |
| Cefotetan | : | 2 mg |
| Colistin sulfate | : | 20 mg |
| Cycloheximide | : | 400 mg |
| Fosfomycin | : | 10 mg |
| Ethanol | : | 5 ml |
| Sterile distilled water | : | 5 ml |

Dissolve the above ingredients and sterilize by filtration.

(iii) Oxford medium

After cooling the medium base (1 L), add the antimicrobial supplement (10 ml) to prepare the complete Oxford medium and dispense in sterile petri dishes.

### 19.2.3 Procedure

Take 25 g of minced sample and add to 225 ml UVM-I enrichment broth and incubate at 30➡C for 24 h.

After inoculation, transfer 0.1 ml inoculum from UVM-I to 9 ml UVM-II and incubate for 24 h at 30➡C.

From UVM-II inoculate a loopful of the enriched sample on Oxford medium plate and incubate at 30➡C for 48 h.

Examine the plate for the appearance of characteristics esculin-positive colonies which are olive-green in colour surrounded by a black halo.

Pick up representative colonies from the suspected ones for confirmation by morphological, cultural and biochemical tests.

### 19.2.4 Observations and recording of results

Observe and record the presence and characteristics of suspected colonies.

Record the results of morphological, cultural and biochemical tests.

Match the results of the tests with features of *L. monocytogenes*.

Decide whether the isolated organism is *Listeria* or not.

### 19.2.5 Interpretation

According to the Food Safety and Standards Regulations (2011), *Listeria* should be absent in 25 g sample of frozen beef, mutton, goat and buffalo meat.

**Record sheet - Detection of *Listeria* species in meat**

| Sample detail | Isolate No. (Colony characteristics) | Gram's reaction/ morphology | Motility | Catalase | Oxidase | MR | VP | Acid production from carbohydrates | | | | CAMP test | | β- haemolysis | Interpretation |
|---|---|---|---|---|---|---|---|---|---|---|---|---|---|---|---|
| | | | | | | | | D-mannitol | L-Rhamnose | D-Xylose | α- methyl-d-mannoside | *S. aureus* | *R. equi* | | |
| | | | | | | | | | | | | | | | |
| | | | | | | | | | | | | | | | |
| | | | | | | | | | | | | | | | |
| | | | | | | | | | | | | | | | |
| | | | | | | | | | | | | | | | |
| | | | | | | | | | | | | | | | |
| | | | | | | | | | | | | | | | |
| | | | | | | | | | | | | | | | |
| | | | | | | | | | | | | | | | |
| | | | | | | | | | | | | | | | |
| | | | | | | | | | | | | | | | |
| | | | | | | | | | | | | | | | |
| | | | | | | | | | | | | | | | |
| | | | | | | | | | | | | | | | |
| | | | | | | | | | | | | | | | |

## 19.3 Enumeration of *Staphylococcus aureus* in meat and meat products

Staphylococci constitute leading cause of foodborne gastroenteritis. The enterotoxin produced by the organisms in food is responsible for the disease. The growth of the toxigenic organisms leads to toxin production in food. Large number of staphylococci thus give rise to the suspicion of presence of pre-formed enterotoxin in food. Hence, the organism should not be present in meat and meat products beyond the permissible limit.

### 19.3.1 Apparatus

| | |
|---|---|
| Petri dishes with culture medium | Sterile pipettes |
| Test tubes | Test tube rack |
| Spreader (L-shaped glass rod) | Beaker |
| Incubator at 37°C | Water bath at 45°C |
| Burner | Marking pen |

### 19.3.2 Culture medium/ reagents

(a) Baired-Parker's agar medium

It is prepared as detailed in Section 8.1.2.

(b) Normal saline solution (diluent)

### 19.3.3 Procedure

Prepare serial dilutions of 25 g sample of the product.

Inoculate Baird-Parker agar medium plates in duplicate with 0.1 ml of the sample dilutions by surface plating.

Incubate the plates at 37°C for 48 hours.

### 19.3.4 Observations and recording of results

Same as given in Section 8.1.4

### 19.3.5 Interpretation

The quality of meat products and sea foods can be evaluated on the basis of Food Safety and Standards Regulations (2011) given in Table 18.1 and Table 18.2.

**Record sheet -** Enumeration of *Staphylococcus aureus* in meat and meat products

| Sample No. | Dilution | Colony count | | | Dilution factor | cfu/g | Interpretation |
|---|---|---|---|---|---|---|---|
| | | Plate I | Plate II | Average | | | |
| | $10^{-1}$ | | | | $10^{1}$ | | |
| | $10^{-2}$ | | | | $10^{2}$ | | |
| | $10^{-3}$ | | | | $10^{3}$ | | |
| | $10^{-4}$ | | | | $10^{4}$ | | |
| | $10^{-5}$ | | | | $10^{5}$ | | |
| | $10^{-6}$ | | | | $10^{6}$ | | |
| | $10^{-1}$ | | | | $10^{1}$ | | |
| | $10^{-2}$ | | | | $10^{2}$ | | |
| | $10^{-3}$ | | | | $10^{3}$ | | |
| | $10^{-4}$ | | | | $10^{4}$ | | |
| | $10^{-5}$ | | | | $10^{5}$ | | |
| | $10^{-6}$ | | | | $10^{6}$ | | |
| | $10^{-1}$ | | | | $10^{1}$ | | |
| | $10^{-2}$ | | | | $10^{2}$ | | |
| | $10^{-3}$ | | | | $10^{3}$ | | |
| | $10^{-4}$ | | | | $10^{4}$ | | |
| | $10^{-5}$ | | | | $10^{5}$ | | |
| | $10^{-6}$ | | | | $10^{6}$ | | |

Module 20

# Identification and differentiation of meat species

Substitution of meat of a particular species of animal with that of another species or mislabeling meat is a fraudulent practice and is considered adulteration. It is objectionable and amounts to cheating of the consumer by passing to him the meat of less expensive species at higher price. It may also hurt the religious sentiments of the people because some particular types of meat are not acceptable to Muslims, Hindus and Jews. Mislabeled meat may also lead to health implications in the form of hypersensitivity reactions in the people having allergy to a particular species.

It is, therefore, necessary sometimes to identify the species of origin of meat. There are several methods to identify and differentiate the meat of different species of animals. These include differentiation based on anatomical features and physical, chemical, biochemical and biological methods.

Identification of food animal species is relatively simple when carcass is intact but it becomes somewhat difficult if carcasses are already processed and gross organs and skin are not available for inspection. Sometimes intact carcass is also difficult to differentiate when it is replaced by the carcass of same size and shape of other species of poor quality meat. Unscrupulous traders take advantage of this situation in many ways.

## 20.1 Identification of carcasses of different species on the basis of anatomical features

Observe the colour, texture and odour of meat. The colour of buffalo meat is darker and coarse than in beef. There is goaty smell in chevon particularly in male goats

Observe the bones for particular characters of different species.

Observe the colour, consistency and distribution of fat. Fat in beef is yellowish while that in buffalo meat is creamy white. In cattle and buffalo, fat is uniformly distributed within muscle tissues (marbling) while in pigs it is present subcutaneously in large amount without intermixing with flesh.

Observe the vertebral column in the carcass and identify the carcass with the help of following Table.

| Species | Cervical | Thoracic | Lumbar | Sacral | Coccygeal |
|---|---|---|---|---|---|
| Ox | 7 | 13 | 6 | 5 | 18-20 |
| Sheep and Goat | 7 | 13 | 6 | 4 | 16-18 |
| Pig | 7 | 14-15 | 6-7 | 4 | 20-23 |
| Horse | 7 | 18 | 6 | 5 | 15-21 |
| Rabbit | 7 | 12 | 7-8 | 3-4 | 14-20 |
| Chicken | 15-17 | 7 | 14 Lumbar + sacral (Fused synsacrum) | | 5-6 Pygostyle (fused caudal vertebrae) |

## 20.2 Differentiation of sheep and goat carcasses

Differentiate sheep and goat carcass with the help of features given in the following Table.

| Feature | Sheep | Goat |
|---|---|---|
| Flesh | Pale red colour, fine texture | Dark red colour, coarse texture, goaty odour, |
| Subcutaneous tissue | Not sticky | Sticky, hair may be adhered |
| Back and withers | Round, more flesh | Sharp, less flesh |
| Thorax | Barrel shaped chest | Laterally flattened narrow chest |
| Scapula | Scapula short and broad, superior spine bent back and thickened | Scapula has distinct neck, spine straight and narrow |
| Radius | Length 1.5 times of metacarpus | Longer, length twice of metacarpus |
| Legs | Shorter | Longer |
| Sacrum | Lateral borders thickened in form of rolls | Lateral border thin and sharp |
| Tail | Thicker and tucked between hind legs | Thinner and away from carcass |
| Kidney fat | Lacking | Abundant |

## 20.3 Differentiation of horse and cattle carcasses

Differentiate carcass of horse from that of cattle with the help of following features.

| Feature | Horse | Cattle |
|---|---|---|
| Muscular development of hind quarters | More | Less |
| Thoracic cavity | Long | Short |
| Rib count | 18 pairs | 13 pairs |
| Shape of rib cage | Narrow, more curved | Broader, less curved |
| Ulna | Extends only half way down the radius | More developed, reaches the carpus |
| Flesh | Dark bluish red | No bluish tinge |

**Record sheet** – Identification of carcass/meat

| Type of sample | Features | Identification |
|---|---|---|
| | | |
| | | |
| | | |
| | | |
| | | |

Module 21

# Inspection of abattoirs, meat processing plants, marketing centers and food service establishments

Quality of meat is greatly influenced by the hygienic practices and sanitary conditions in the abattoirs, meat processing plants and marketing centers. The quality of meat also depends upon the location as well as construction plan of these establishments, type of equipments and several environmental factors. Failure to pay due attention to any of these aspects in a food establishment is bound to result in deterioration in product quality. It may either lead to reduced shelf life of the product or may cause public health threat.

Therefore, besides strict ante-mortem and post-mortem inspection in the abattoir, critical systematic inspection of food establishments is also very essential to ensure hygienic and safe food supply to the consumers.

## 21.1 Visual inspection

Carry out visual inspection and collect specimens for laboratory analysis wherever required and record the observations.

Evaluate the status and recommend corrective measures where required.

### 21.1.1 Building

| | |
|---|---|
| Location | Surroundings |
| Layout plan | Design |
| Space | Floors |
| Walls | Ceiling |
| Doors | Windows |
| Working surfaces | Pipelines |
| Drainage | Ventilation |
| Lighting | Water points |
| Facility for cleaning and disinfection | |

### 21.1.2 Cleaning and sanitation status

### 21.1.3 Equipment

| | |
|---|---|
| Adequacy | Design |
| Mechanization | Ease of operation |
| Ease of cleaning | Maintenance status |
| Hygiene of meat processing equipments | Safety of operators |

### 21.1.4 Hygienic processing of meat

### 21.1.5 Pest control

### 21.1.6 Facilities for workers hygiene

### 21.1.7 Personal hygiene status of workers

### 21.1.8 Health status of workers

### 21.1.9 Water supply

### 21.1.10 Air quality

### 21.1.11 Disposal of waste

### 21.1.12 Process verification reports (Past 7 days)

## 21.2 Laboratory examinations of environmental samples

- Collection of water sample for bacteriological examination
- Air sampling for bacteriological examination
- Collection of swabs from equipments and working surfaces for bacteriological examination

## 21.3 Personal hygiene and health status check up of workers

- Visual check up
- Collection of swabs from hands, nose, throat, skin etc.

**Record sheet -** Inspection of abattoirs/meat processing plants/marketing centers and food service establishments

**A) Visual inspection**

| Sr. No. | Parameter | Compliance (Mark ↗ in case of compliance and X in case of non-compliance) | Corrective action, in case of non-compliance | Remarks |
|---|---|---|---|---|
| 1. | Building | | | |
| | Location | | | |
| | Surroundings | | | |
| | Layout plan | | | |

| | | | | |
|---|---|---|---|---|
| | Design | | | |
| | Space | | | |
| | Floors | | | |
| | Walls | | | |
| | Ceiling | | | |
| | Working surfaces | | | |
| | Pipelines | | | |
| | Doors | | | |
| | Windows | | | |
| | Drainage | | | |
| | Ventilation | | | |
| | Lighting | | | |
| | Water points | | | |
| | Facility for cleaning and disinfection | | | |
| 2. | Cleaning and sanitation status | | | |
| 3. | Equipment | | | |
| | Adequacy | | | |
| | Design | | | |
| | Mechanization | | | |
| | Ease of operation | | | |
| | Ease of cleaning | | | |
| | Maintenance status | | | |
| | Hygiene of meat processing equipments | | | |
| | Safety of operators | | | |
| 4. | Hygienic processing of meat | | | |

| | | | | |
|---|---|---|---|---|
| 5. | Pest control | | | |
| 6. | Facilities for workers hygiene | | | |
| 7. | Personal hygiene status of workers | | | |
| 8. | Health status of workers | | | |
| 9. | Water supply | | | |
| 10. | Air quality | | | |
| 11. | Disposal of waste | | | |
| 12. | Process verification reports (Past 7 days) | | | |

**B) Laboratory evaluation**

| **Sample No.** | **Details of sample** | **Microbiological test and result** | **Remarks/Corrective action** |
|---|---|---|---|
| Water | | | |
| | | | |
| | | | |
| | | | |
| Air | | | |
| | | | |
| | | | |
| | | | |
| Swabs | | | |
| | | | |
| | | | |
| | | | |

**C) Personal hygiene and health status of workers**

| Observations on personal hygiene of workers | Observations on health status of workers |
|---|---|
| | |

# Index